Charles Dickens' Australia

Book One
Convict Stories

CHARLES DICKENS.

Charles Dickens' Australia
Selected essays from *Household Words*
1850–1859

Book One
Convict Stories

Researched and presented by
Margaret Mendelawitz

SYDNEY UNIVERSITY PRESS

Published 2011 by SYDNEY UNIVERSITY PRESS
University of Sydney Library
sydney.edu.au/sup

Sydney University Press
Fisher Library F03, University of Sydney,
NSW 2006 AUSTRALIA
Email: sup.info@sydney.edu.au

National Library of Australia Cataloguing-in-Publication entry

Mendelawitz, Margaret.
Charles Dickens' Australia : selected essays from Household Words 1850 - 1859 :
    convict stories / Researched and presented by Margaret Mendelawitz.
9781920898670 (pbk. : bk. 1)
9781920899271 (set)
Includes bibliographical references.
A823.4

Cover image: Prisoners under escort for Bathurst Gaol, watercolour by George Lacy
(c. 1816–1878?). Image courtesy of National Library of Australia, pic-an3103631-v.

Frontispiece: Portrait of Charles Dickens engraved by Robert Graves (1798–1873)
after painting (1859) by William Powell Frith (1819–1909). Engraving published in
the second volume of John Forster's *The Life of Dickens* (London: Chapman and Hall,
1872–74).

Cover design by Court Williams, University Publishing Service
Printed in Australia

Contents

This book contains stories and articles written over 150 years ago, and from a predominantly Anglo-Celtic perspective. It contains terms and descriptions that we would not consider acceptable of people and cultural groups today. Women, the Irish, Chinese and Australian Aborigines are described in biased, racist, stereotypical or otherwise less than flattering terms. As Margaret Mendelawitz notes in her Introduction, Dickens himself held conservative views about women and their ability to overcome their 'lesser nature'.

We ask that you remember this as you read the stories, and encourage you to work towards a more positive understanding of the different groups that make up our community.

Foreword

The Australian gold rushes were, in the eyes of millions of Europeans of the 1850s, the most astonishing episode they could read about. Here was gold, lying on or near the surface of the ground in enormous quantities, and available to the first person who could dig a shallow hole with pick, crowbar and shovel. Some of the richest nuggets of gold ever found were on the Victorian goldfields. It was no wonder that emigration from the British Isles to this El Dorado was on an unprecedented scale.

The London magazine *Household Words* conveyed to thousands of literate homes the news and atmosphere, the strangeness and the excitement, of Australian daily life before and during the gold rushes. Two of the best writers living in Australia—they had arrived especially to dig gold or to watch it being dug—contributed prose and poems to *Household Words*. While the magazine had a focus far wider than this one country, it liked Australia to be one of its major themes.

Between 1850 and 1859 more than one hundred of its articles and many of its poems were about this country. At a time when Australia's white population was less than one million, and the local weeklies and monthlies were few and precarious, this high-circulation English magazine offered a freshly washed window on Australia. The window was unusual because it was controlled by the most celebrated English novelist, Charles Dickens. One of his novels, *Hard Times*, first appeared as a serial in this magazine. Dickens rewrote or edited many of the articles on Australian themes. Such was his fascination with this country that he encouraged or permitted his young sons to emigrate and take up pastoral lands. The older became a member of parliament in NSW, representing an outback seat.

Margaret Mendelawitz has collected, and given the background to, the prose and verse assembled here: she even knows how much the authors were paid, to the nearest shilling. We can see what English readers learned about Australia in those mid-century years: the long voyage and its dangers, the life of convicts and copper miners before the gold rushes, and the hazardous life in the bush: it published Louisa Meredith's long poem on the little child that disappeared. We experience through *Household Words* the jubilant streets of Melbourne when it was the busiest port for the new goldfields, the slow journey on foot to the diggings, the makeshift gold towns themselves, the life of migrating women at sea and on land, the eccentricities of the new-rich, and scores of other topics. Three stories—one of which is fictional but historically vital—hinge on the terrible bushfires of 6 February 1851. Known as Black Thursday it had virtually been wiped from the nation's collective memory before the bushfires of February 2009, Black Saturday resurrected it.

Some of these authors had not seen Australia but winnowed private letters and newspaper accounts. On the other hand 'Orion' Horne was the only English writer with a literary reputation who had settled here up to that time, and his stories of what he saw and heard are compelling. All in all, this is a rare anthology and mirror of Australia when it was glamorous and exotic for potential British emigrants, and enticed them here as never before.

Geoffrey Blainey
Melbourne, May 2010

Introduction
Margaret Mendelawitz

The articles, poems and narratives contained in this anthology were published by Charles Dickens in his weekly periodical, *Household Words*, between the years 1850 and 1859.

Today, Dickens is recognised as the foremost English novelist of the Victorian era, and at the time was probably the most famous writer in the English-speaking world. His many volumes include such works as *The Pickwick Papers, Oliver Twist, Martin Chuzzlewit, Bleak House, Great Expectations* and short stories such as the much-loved *A Christmas Carol.*

His first novel was published when he was in his mid-twenties and his reputation and standing as a writer continued to grow over the next thirty years. As a novelist Dickens was much more than a writer and entertainer. He was on one hand able to charm and delight his audience, while at the same time communicating his ideas on a great variety of subjects—often concerning ordinary people and frequently exposing the shortcomings and seamy nature of the lives of the poor, compared with the lives of the privileged.

He was also a natural journalist and enjoyed the power of being able to speak directly to his audience on subjects that concerned him. In the first edition of *Household Words*, published in England on 30th March 1850, he outlined its governing principles to be—'Principles of Progress and Improvements, of Education, Civil and Religious Liberty, Equal Legislation.'

Household Words proved to be a remarkable periodical that was published during an extraordinary decade in Australian and British history: a decade when the tumultuous effects of the discovery and mining of gold in New South Wales and Victoria were being experienced worldwide. In Britain and Australia the results of increasing attention to issues of social justice were being felt, and around the world, the 'age of capital' had begun.[1] Of the thousands of articles published in *Household Words* in this decade more than one hundred were related to Australia. It is these that are reproduced in this anthology.

Dickens was thirty-eight in 1850 when he began publishing *Household Words*. He had twice tried his hand as editor of other periodicals but had been frustrated by his lack of control over their content. Already an acclaimed author, he was also a journalist of twenty years experience. With a growing family to support, he saw *Household Words* as a way to generate a secure income whilst at the same time to allowing him to continue writing his novels. As a journalist, he had been a parliamentary reporter and had written on election campaigns and public meetings, as well as producing theatre reviews and reports of important dinners.[2] He was known for his 'comic, witty or punchy commentaries on topical subjects'—and in many ways, was a predecessor of today's magazine or newspaper columnist.

He had already proven himself to be a man of action. In 1839, at the age of twenty-seven, he met Baroness Angela Burdette Coutts, said to be the wealthiest woman in England after the Queen. They began to actively and enthusiastically cooperate in a wide range of charitable projects, in particular *Urania Cottage* for the retraining and rehabilitation of fallen women.[3] Dickens was more practical and pragmatic in his approach than Baroness Coutts who was a promoter of abstinence, especially from sex and alcohol. He preferred to teach the women skills and to assist them to migrate to Australia to make a 'new start'. This approach would later on lead him to endorse the work of Caroline Chisholm in the first instalment of *Household Words*.[4]

By 1850, his views on social issues had become clearer and more radical. He announced the aim of *Household Words* as 'the raising up of those that are down, and the general improvement of our social conditions'.[5] His particular concerns were sanitation, education and housing, the lack of which he believed were the root causes of much of the 'disastrous conditions of England'. He was of the opinion that the causes of most of the ills of the world, including disease, crime and social unrest, were as a result of ignorance and neglect. This concern was a recurrent theme in Dickens' earliest writings.

However, his own attitudes were a mixture of conservatism and radicalism that persisted throughout his life. For instance, he was steadfastly conservative in his views regarding the place of women in society, where he maintained their natural place was firmly at home and other activities should not, in any way, take priority over the needs of the children. Indeed, he draws a metaphor to this in his novel *Bleak House*, (1853) with Mrs Jellyby, a do-gooder who neglects her children in order to do her charitable works. Mrs Jellyby is said to have been modelled on the social reformer Caroline Chisholm: yet, at the same time, he was endorsing Chisholm's charitable work in assisting families to emigrate to Australia. In addition, his own personal and family life was far from the virtuous model he projected as the ideal in his novels; he ultimately left his wife Catherine, taking their children with him, whilst maintaining a relationship with another woman, Ellen Ternan. His own travels, and the frantic pace of life he led, would, in today's society, constitute neglect of family duties.

Amongst humans, story is our unique and most powerful form of communication. It provides a window through which we can view the lives of others and so gain insight into their thoughts and subsequent actions. Topics can be introduced to readers in a range of ways aimed at informing them, raising their interest and fostering concern. Unconstrained, the story can move through time and place, linking the present with the past, engaging the reader at new emotional and experiential levels. By stimulating the imagination the well-constructed story facilitates contemplation and reflection on the human condition, in a way that indeed may be transformative.

Charles Dickens well understood the power of story. The narrative, more than simply providing entertainment for the reader (or listener), has the ability to transform: to enable the reader to enter the story and, moreover, for the story to enter the reader, often in a profound and lasting way. He also preferred the power of the popular press, rather than writing for the more scholarly publications. He wanted to be able to express important ideas by communicating through high-quality journalism in an inexpensive, readily available weekly.

Dickens wanted to affect, and hence change, the reader through story. He knew that hectoring and preaching more often had the effect of disengaging rather than engaging an audience. He wanted to enlighten and reform his society and to make a significant contribution to the cultural debate. He set out to do this by informative and influential storytelling, through the lively blending of fact and fiction, set against the realities of social conditions of the times.

Dickens disliked sermonising of any form and was especially repelled by religions that stressed adherence to dogma rather than compassion and goodwill—he was a man of religious convictions yet rarely went to church.[6] Dickens was by nature neither an ideologue nor a revolutionary. He was wary of trade unions while still sympathetic to the conditions of workers. Yet he believed in strict prison sentences rather than focusing on reform.

By 1850 he was already a man with a high profile having earlier taken a very public stand against the practice of public hangings. Dickens was appalled by the spectacle of public executions which had turned into a form of entertainment for the masses. When they were abolished in Britain in 1868 he was 'remembered as one of the great advocates of this change.'[7] He was against the social isolation of prisoners which he considered cruel and inhumane; and vehemently against slavery, which he had witnessed first-hand in America.[8] He considered that transported prisoners were virtually slave labourers and he strongly opposed this abuse.

Dickens had a great curiosity about other societies and other lands and had a great love of travel. He visited North America on two occasions and at various times had toured Italy, Switzerland, France, Ireland and Scotland. He published books on his American travels and on Europe. He was a keen observer of French culture, government and history and after his separation from his wife spent a large amount of his time living in France. His novel *A Tale of Two Cities* (1859) was set in France. Dickens' inquisitiveness and intense interest in faraway lands, including Australia, is mirrored in many of the articles in *Household Words*: it is also occasionally reflected in his novels when a character's fate was to find salvation in Australia, as did Magwitch in *Great Expectations* and Mr Micawber in *David Copperfield*.

Apart from providing the financial security Dickens was seeking, *Household Words* was to be a vehicle for promoting his ideas of reform and a way of forming a closer relationship with his readers. It was not to be a high-brow intellectual periodical. Above all he wanted to reach and entertain the masses and, at the same time, help shape discussion and debate on the important social questions of the time. His aim was to engage some of the best and most entertaining writers to produce a range of stories and narratives, as well as poetry—'good' poetry that would appeal to ordinary readers. However, Dickens' assessment of what was 'good' poetry was not always shared in educated circles.

The stories in *Household Words* were to have a clear purpose or focus which Dickens himself was to guide and influence. He intended to instruct, educate and assist the reader to make judgements on a very wide range of subjects. The articles were to be 'compilations' such as essays, reviews, letters, theatrical criticism, which were to be as 'amusing' as possible.[9] The writers were to be well paid, with a clear understanding of what was expected of them.

In setting down his governing philosophy for *Household Words*, and the range of subjects he wished to explore, Dickens wrote to his close friend and future biographer John Forster:

> Now to bind all this together, and to get a character established as it were which any of the writers may maintain without difficulty, I want to suppose a certain *Shadow* which may go into any place by sunlight, moonlight, starlight , firelight, candlelight, and be in all homes, and all nooks and corners, and be supposed to be cognisant of everything, and go everywhere, without the least difficulty. Which may be the theatre, the Palace, the House of Commons, the Prisons, the Unions, the Churches, on the Railroad, on the Sea, abroad and at home: a kind of semi-omnipresent, intangible creature. I don't think it would do to call the paper the The Shadow: but I want something tacked to that title, to express the notion of its being cheerful, useful, and always welcome Shadow.[10]

Beginning in March 1850, *Household Words* was published weekly for almost a decade. Publication ended in 1859 after a bitter quarrel with his publishers and shareholders in the enterprise, Bradbury and Evans. For the next ten years he published a similar periodical *All The Year Round (AYR)* until his death in 1870. However, *AYR* contained less political journalism and more serialised fiction. Dickens chose the ever competent William Henry Wills to be his principal subeditor of both *Household Words* and *AYR*—a capacity that Wills excelled in for nearly twenty years while carefully managing the day-to-day running of the periodicals. In addition to Dickens and his publishers, the other shareholders were John Forster and William Wills, both of whom wrote many articles for the periodical.

Dickens closely scrutinised each weekly publication, even while abroad, and wrote many of the articles himself. He was concerned that no inaccuracies crept into the pages, writing to Wills, 'nothing can be more damaging to *Household Words* as carelessness about facts. It is a hideous dullness'.[11]

Some of the pieces are what Dickens himself called 'composite' writings: materials he wrote in collaboration with other staff members. The final product was achieved by dividing the task and then flawlessly putting the sections together through meticulous editing. Dickens put an enormous amount of effort into refining the written works so that they appeared to be that of a single author. According to the Dickens scholar Harry Stone the result was that many of these articles are among the 'most carefully planned and polished writings' of Dickens' works.[12]

The same process applied to articles that had been submitted to him by writers who were not staff members or commissioned authors and to the few written by readers. The latter were often prefaced as 'Chip' which often commented on some aspect of a previous article. An example is the article 'Chip: Colonial Patriot',—an extract from a personal letter written to Dickens by John Fawkner, the first European to settle on the site of Melbourne in 1835. Occasionally a full-length article in the form of prose or poetry by a reader was published, but always after receiving a good buff-up from either Dickens or Wills to make it sparkle (and conform). It was not easy to have works published in *Household Words*: in 1854 for example, nearly 900 were submitted by readers and only eleven were printed.[13]

Included in this nucleus of staff writers were two who came to Australia during their time with *Household Words* with Dickens' instruction to send back articles for publication. They were Richard Horne, a salaried staff member who served with William Wills for a time as subeditor, and William Howitt. At another level, was a large group, many of whom were rising new writers at the time. They included Henry Morley, who was on the permanent staff with a salary of five guineas per week, and Samuel Sidney who was a regular contributor. Morley and Sidney both had brothers who spent time in Australia, and wrote articles for *Household Words*.

Other regular contributors included Wilkie Collins, Mrs Elizabeth Gaskell, and many others including Edmund Ollier, James Payn and George Sala, all prominent authors at the time. Though not permanent staff members, they augmented the team by writing on specialised subjects, such as science, medicine, legal matters, shipping and travel. Articles by Ollier, Payn and Sala are included in this anthology. George Sala also came to Australia long after Dickens' death and subsequently coined the aphorism 'Marvellous Melbourne'.[14] Beyond this level there was another group of writers including Elizabeth Barrett Browning, Dinah Maria Mulock, Edmund Yeats, and George Meredith; articles by the latter are included here.

Dickens was much more than editor-in-chief of *Household Words*, preferring to call himself the 'conductor' and he happily received letters and manuscripts addressed to Mr Conductor from hopeful writers from all around the world. By this means, Dickens maintained a direct linkage and close connection to his huge audience of readers—and they in turn provided the raw materials that so often shaped or informed the articles contained in the periodical. Also, and importantly, they informed the characters and settings appearing in his novels.

In addition, and essential for Dickens, he was now successfully able to promote his social concerns with the same action and energy as typified his narratives and novels. The audience was large. As Jane Smiley has said, in relation to his novels written at this time:

> He created a new sort of English novel, one that explores and questions the construction of English culture and society as a whole,

rather than merely certain institutions. Dickens locates the dilemmas and tragedies of his characters in the institutions outside of their control and then analyses how some of the characters fail while others manage to cope.[15]

Except for the novel *Hard Times,* published in serial form in *Household Words,* it was not possible for Dickens to explore major themes in any depth in the short articles contained in *Household Words.* Nevertheless, at the outset Dickens had a clear vision as to the nature of the material to be included in the new periodical, writing to John Forster:

> Upon the selected matter, I have a particular notion. One is that it should always be *a subject.* For example ... A history of Savages, showing the singular respect in which all savages are like each other; and those in which civilized men, under circumstances of difficulty, soonest become like savages. A history of remarkable characters, good and bad, *in* history; to assist the reader's judgement in his observation of men, and in his estimates of the truth of many characters in fiction.[16]

Of the nearly 3000 articles that appeared in *Household Words,* the narrative style was unashamedly middle-class in nature. It was deliberately pitched to capture the attention of the growing number of readers at this level of society. Each issue usually had between five and seven articles of popular interest, on topics such as sanitation, epidemics, education, the treatment of prisoners or children, or men at sea. Other themes covered were history, travel and literature. There was generally a story and an essay, and frequently a poem.

Most, if not all, were couched in a deliberately bright tone in which entertainment was combined with instruction. In an era when Victorian prudery and primness would not allow frank speaking about such things as sewage and filth, Dickens acceded to his public's sensitivities. He paid particular attention to style, and in everything, including the driest of subjects, he demanded brightness. His message once to his editor William Wills was to 'brighten it, brighten it, brighten it!' He also demanded the same from his writers, requiring them to adopt, as Mrs Gaskell termed, a

'Dickensy' style.[17] There was always a lead article each week that set the tone and shape of the articles to follow.

Another distinct characteristic was the provocative introductory paragraphs which were often deliberately clever, ingenious or snappy (often a pun) and intended to entice readers into articles containing serious messages. Dickens desired that the publication become 'the gentle mouthpiece of reform'.[18] As an indication of Dickens' control over subject matter, Martin Fido is very forthright, writing that throughout the life of the journal, Dickens 'could be and was—ruthlessly dictatorial on matters of content and style'. Furthermore, contributors who had not conformed to Dickens' views 'had their work re-written'[19] and regardless of their source, all articles appeared anonymously.

Household Words became extremely popular. It eventually averaged sales of about 40,000 copies per week and at its peak 100,000 copies per week, returning Dickens a good profit and secure income. In addition, he earned money from his novels, said to have been £11,000 from just one novel in the 1850s.[20]

Through *Household Words* Dickens had created the perfect vehicle of good humour and good spirits to reach even the poorest and most distant home. Many articles from *Household Words* were re-published in the Australian press. This was a further opportunity for Australians to see how they were being depicted in the popular press of the time, and conceivably, to influence the way Australians imagined themselves as a society. The reprinted articles would have communicated Dickens' views to a wider audience, providing Dickens with a unique opportunity to alter and shape public opinion in a progressive and rapidly developing country.

Of the articles reproduced in this volume, all are related in some way to Australia. What makes this collection unique is that they were all published between 1850 and 1859, the decisive decade in which gold was discovered in New South Wales and Victoria. These subsequent events were to not only to transform colonial Australia economically and socially, but changed how the colonies were perceived by the world at large.

To have so many articles published in one single periodical under the strict guiding hand of Charles Dickens is unparalleled in Australian literature.

To have such a clear understanding of the guiding principles of the editor-in-chief is surely without precedent. Dickens obtained access to a wealth of knowledge from information and feedback from his Australian readership, as well as from his regular writers, such as Horne and Howitt. These staff writers, like so many people around the globe, were attracted to Australia by the excitement of gold. Thus, at the outset, they were commissioned by Dickens to record their journeys and their experiences for the readers of *Household Words*.

Many of these articles display a freshness and sense of drama we are familiar with today. But in a world where even Scotland was yet to be fully mapped (1862),[21] and with the interior of Australia unknown, uncharted and exotic, they were breaking new ground. They are, of course, not all eyewitness accounts. Many are representations based on fact, while some are serious critiques about shipping to Australia, 'We Mariners of England'; the plight of emigrants on board ships, 'A Diggers Diary'; or of living conditions in Melbourne, 'Canvass Town [sic]'. All are part of the body of literature that emerged with the gold rushes, literature that helped to shape a new way of thinking about life in colonial Australia. Australian life was now depicted as thrilling and different with an exciting future ahead, a country standing apart from its stark convict beginnings. Life in the new world was being presented as offering opportunities for a new start, radically different from that in early industrial Britain. Australia had just won the golden lottery, and the world was fascinated.

There are other snippets of information that make this collection so valuable. For example the amount each writer was paid varied: staff received a salary, while articles submitted regardless of the source were paid according to the piece and to the numbers of columns printed in the original publication. Interestingly poetry was always paid at a much higher rate than prose.

Biographical information about each of the contributors, including a list of their articles related to Australia, can be found at the end of the text; the biographies of each of the contributors providing yet another layer of insight into the articles. In many instances this is by no means a complete list of the writers' works, for many of these contributors wrote extensively for *Household Words* on subjects unrelated to Australia.

Of the thirty-five individual authors who contributed articles relating to Australia, by far the greatest proportion (twenty-one) had either lived in Australia for lengthy periods of time, or were permanent settlers. Of the latter, nine were either journalists or regular contributors to Australian publications, with two (Fawkner and Vincent) also colonial newspaper proprietors.

In addition, eight of the contributors published books about Australia—John Capper, Caroline Chisholm, William Howitt, John Lang, Louisa Meredith, brothers John and Samuel Sidney, and the Rev. William Ullathorne. In some instances, as in the case of John Lang, articles first published in *Household Words* formed the basis of a subsequent book.

Eric Hobsbawm has written in *The Age of Capital* that the coincidence of gold discoveries in California in 1848–49, and in Australia, marked the foundation of the 'global industrial economy' and the start of a 'single world history'.[22] Gold was the spark that ignited a sudden burst of mass migration, largely to America, and to a far lesser extent to Australia. Even so, in the space of ten years Australia's population trebled, while the population of Victoria rose by a factor of seven—a state of affairs unimaginable today.[23]

Gold transformed economies, created new markets and led to a world-wide economic surge. Australia, with the vast riches being claimed from its soil, was the powerhouse behind much of this. In the next decade this chain of events saw a new word, 'capitalism' entering into the economic and political vocabulary, and the growth and interdependence of the single world economy.[24]

As Geoffrey Blainey has written:

> In the year 1853 Australia bought 15 per cent of the total value of goods exported from Great Britain, the world's largest exporter. Britain's exports to the new gold countries of North America and Australia increased by 271 per cent in the years 1846–53; and in the same period Britain's exports to the rest of the world increased by only 21 per cent. There is evidence that California and then Australia had such purchasing power that they largely revived the sick economy of Britain, which in turn sent a chain reaction of prosperity around much of the civilized world.[25]

Apart from gold's great economic benefit, it was the prize that anyone with a bit of luck and capital might win. Australia benefited in many ways, but especially by the people it attracted, mostly young, physically fit men, frequently educated to some degree and willing to be adaptable, resourceful and to have a go! During the height of the gold rush up to 300 ships could be at anchor in Port Phillip Bay at any one time. Sailors deserted their ships and sea-going mates remained trusted mates at the diggings—thus helping to cement forever this term in the Australian idiom.

This melting pot of energetic young men from every class and rank of society helped to shape Australia's future politics. They helped to create a modern sense of justice, uncommon in their countries of origin, which revolutionised institutions and benefited the social and economic transition of Australia into a modern developing economy. This decade saw the granting of the eight-hour day for some workers and, in the decades to follow, manhood suffrage, payment for members of Parliament and the secret ballot; the list goes on.

Many of the articles published in *Household Words* capture the excitement of the times and many foreshadow the personal despair of hopeful immigrants. As a body of literature for the masses, *Household Words* does not set out to explore Australian society or culture as a whole. Very few articles reflect local politics but they do manage to highlight a range of issues, personal triumphs and tragedies reflecting the dramatic shift in the British perception of Australia in this extraordinary decade. Originally perceived to be a distant colonial outpost of convicts, farmers and squatters, Australia came to be depicted as a place of adventure, wealth and limitless future.

But these stories are literature, not history. They are historically enlightening and their value is in their ability to educate readers about the social and economic development of 19th-century Australia. This value does not depend on them being the literal truth, as even the most conscientious organising of facts will not necessarily convey absolute truth. What they do well is to show that there are all sorts of ways to express and develop important ideas—a concept which still holds resonance in today's multimedia society.

As a collection they demonstrate the complementary nature of storytelling between the writing of history and fiction. The stories in *Household Words* frequently draw a fine line between fact and fiction, giving voice to characters and events that could easily go unrecognised and unrecorded. In many ways they exemplify the fundamental problem encountered by historians through the ages of how to separate and present fact, fiction, myth and truth. Moreover, they demonstrate how to overcome the difficulties of bringing Australian history to life to make it more engaging, accessible and meaningful to the reader.

In their own way these articles aptly illustrate, through storytelling, that Australian history does not consist of a single narrative of events; they serve to illustrate that all history is in reality a rich layering of overlapping and often connected narratives, experienced by individuals, groups, communities and the nation as a whole.

Notes on Presentation of Articles
The topics included in this anthology are diverse. The articles have been subjectively placed into five general areas to make them more readily accessible. It is acknowledged that some of the articles may contain themes common to other sections; as much as possible they are organised chronologically and details of their date of publication are attached.

Convict Stories (**Book One**) Conviction and court processes; conditions of prisons; and finally, treatment of convicts until conditional or final pardon received. The articles cover convicts on board ship, on Norfolk Island and mainland Australia and Tasmania, including prison hulks in Victoria.

Immigration (**Book Two**) What to take to Australia and what to expect; where to get good information about immigration; how to choose a vessel to sail on.

Frontier Stories (**Book Three**) Life in the bush. Farmers, squatters, explorers, Aborigines, bushrangers, cattle drives, floods, fire and other vignettes from everyday life.

Mining and Gold (**Book Four**) Copper mining in South Australia. How the discovery of gold beckoned people from all over the world to the gold diggings. The astonishing effect gold had on individuals, the exploding population and colonial life in general. Stories of sailors deserting their vessels, Chinese immigrants and men and women of all ranks of society hoping to strike it rich. Life and death at the diggings, fashion and frivolity.

Maritime Conditions (**Book Five**) The need to improve the desperate conditions endured by seamen; the need for a faster route for ships to travel; steam ships; conditions on board for passengers on the long hazardous sea voyage to Australia. Also, a whaling story and much more.

Usually the original spellings and styles are retained. Occasionally the text has been altered in a small way, such as where spelling is inconsistent, for example when the archaic, trowsers and modern spelling of trousers is used interchangeably in one article, and when obvious typographical errors have occurred. Where 'pounds' was indicated as for instance 5*l*, instead of £5, it has been changed to be represented by the modern £ sign. Some of the very long paragraphs have been broken to assist the modern reader more used to shorter paragraphs, in each case the symbol ˜ has been inserted to indicate where the break occurs. Names of ships, newspapers and journals have been italicised. Now and then a word (or so) in square brackets has been added to aid comprehension.

While Dickens did not like footnotes to any degree (he referred to them as hiccoughs), there were a few in the original text which have been retained. In addition to these original footnotes a number of additional ones have been added for the benefit of the modern reader, such as, to define parts of ships, types of carriages and other modes of transport. Also, in the case where the word has little or no meaning in the modern context: for instance the use of the word plucks for offal.

Biographical notes for all contributors have been included at the end of each volume. These augment the reader's understanding of how Australia was being depicted in popular literature of the era. These biographical details reveal the rich diversity and depth of the Australian experience of the contributors.

Charles Dickens, 'The Conductor' had indeed chosen a remarkable group of individuals who successfully met his aims and hopes for *Household Words.*

Notes

[1] Hobsbawm, Eric, *The Age of Capital: 1848-1875*, p.13.

[2] Rosen, Michael, *Dickens: His Work and his World*, pp. 31–32.

[3] Smiley, Jane, *Charles Dickens*, p.18.

[4] Ackroyd, Peter, *Dickens*, pp. 617–23.

[5] Lohrli, Anne, *Household Words: Table of Contents*, p. 4.

[6] Murray, Brian, *Charles Dickens*, pp. 28–29.

[7] Fido, Martin, *Charles Dickens*. p. 74.

[8] Stone, Harry, *Charles Dickens' Uncollected Writings from Household Words*, pp. 433–42.

[9] Forster, John, *The Life of Charles Dickens: The Fireside Dickens*, p. 555.

[10] Forster, *ibid.,* p. 556.

[11] Ackroyd, Peter, *Dickens*, p. 623.

[12] Stone, *op. cit.*, p. 43.

[13] Hobsbaum, Phillip, *A Reader's Guide to Charles Dickens*, p. 128.

[14] Flannery, Tim, *The Birth of Melbourne*, p. 326.

[15] Smiley, *op. cit.*, p. 97.

[16] Forster, *op. cit.*, p. 555.

[17] Smiley, *op. cit.*, p. 92.

[18] Letter to Wills, March 6, 1850. cf., Una Pope-Hennessy, *Charles Dickens*, p. 302.

[19] Fido, *op. cit.*, p. 68.

[20] Ford, George H., *Dictionary of Literary Biography: University of Rochester.*

[21] Hobsbawm, Eric, *op. cit.*, p. 68.

[22] Hobsbawm, Eric, *op. cit.,* p. 63.

[23] Bate, Weston, *Victorian Gold Rushes*, pp. 8–9.

[24] Hobsbawm, Eric, *op. cit.*, p. 79.

[25] Blainey, Geoffrey, *The Rush That Never Ended*, p. 62.

" Familiar in their Mouths as HOUSEHOLD WORDS."—Shakespeare.

HOUSEHOLD WORDS.

A Weekly Journal.

CONDUCTED BY

CHARLES DICKENS.

VOLUME I.

LONDON:

WARD, LOCK, AND TYLER,

WARWICK HOUSE, PATERNOSTER ROW, E.C.

Book One
Convict Stories

1
Among the Shallows
James Payn and Henry Morley

Disparity in sentencing for petty larceny—from short prison sentences to transportation.

Volume: 8 Number: 189 Pages: 233–35

Date: November 5, 1853

Fee: 1 pound 11 shillings and 6 pence for 4 ½ Columns.

We trust there may be found no Star-chamber[1] matter in it, but we have a belief that justice sometimes runs aground among the Shallows.[2] In spite of their lineage, descended as they all are from Robert Shallow, esquire, in the County of Gloucester, Justice of Peace and coram—ay, and cust alorum—ay, and ratolorum, and gentleman born, who wrote himself armigero.[3]

When transportation was a ready punishment for all offenders there was odd-handed justice administered at quarter sessions, and in other high

---

[1] Star-chamber: relates to an executive body that holds closed meetings (not subject to legal requirements) where the outcomes of the meetings are often a foregone conclusion.

[2] 'Among the Shallows': Robert Shallow is a country justice appearing in Shakespeare's *The Merry Wives of Windsor* and *Henry the Fourth* (both written in 1598). His entry speech includes the statement 'I will make a star chamber of it'.

[3] Corum, cust-alorum and ratolorum are corruptions of legal Latin terms, and armigero, (Latin, to bear arms) are used by three characters in Act 1 of *The Merry Wives of Windsor* to describe Robert Shallow. The authors are suggesting that the low standards of country judges mimic Shallow's behaviour, and question whether sentences to transportation might well have been analogous to those from a Star-chamber.

judicial places. There used to be a power given by the law to transport any one for larceny who had been once convicted of a felony. The power was one that required much tact and delicacy in the handling, and anything that requires tact and delicacy in the handling, it was natural to entrust to the keeping of the Shallow family, just as it might be natural for any man dealing extensively in glass and china to engage an elephant or bull as shop-walker. Such animals would promptly call attention to the delicacy of the wares.

So far as that last matter is concerned, we will take the part of elephant, and show some of the delicacies of the law. In the first place, it is well known that a true Shallow—honorary or stipendiary—must be terrible; 'tis in his blood: rogues and particularly vagabonds—who are the worst kind of rogues—must tremble when he clears his throat. He knows that what is worth doing is worth doing well; he does not like half measures of punishment; seven years' transportation is the lowest figure at which he can be said to do business with any degree of pleasure, and if a prisoner be rude, or should call Verges a pig, or fail in a just admiration of the court, his worship is ready to say another seven, make the term fourteen, and close the bargain. Thus Colonel Jebb informed the public in his report for eighteen hundred and fifty, that 'During the last ten years there has not been an average of more than ten or twelve persons sentenced to a longer period than two years' imprisonment, and less than four hundred and fifty to two years and above one year; whereas the number sentenced to periods of seven years' and ten years' transportation has varied from three thousand nine hundred and twenty-one to two thousand two hundred and twenty-six.' Furthermore we may add, that by the tables of criminal offenders for the year last closed, it appears that only three persons were sentenced to imprisonment for periods exceeding two years, and less than six hundred were imprisoned for two years or between one and two. But there were two or three thousand transported from seven to ten years, and of those eight hundred and forty-seven were so sentenced for simple acts of larceny. So we see what sort of sentencing the Shallows used to relish, and the great sweep lately made upon the transportation system must, it is to be feared, leave them as disconsolate as an alderman after a waiter has run off with his unfinished callipash and callipee.[4]

Now, let us look under the surface, and ascertain if we can how justice is justified in these her ways. We take up an 'Abstract Return of Persons tried for Larceny at Courts of Quarter Sessions for the Counties of Berks, Dorset, Somerset, Southampton (including the Isle of Wight), Sussex, and Wiltshire, in the year eighteen hundred and forty-nine.' Here we read that in the county of Berkshire four persons, for thefts to the amount of eighteen and six-pence, received transportation to the amount of eight-and-twenty years; that in Dorsetshire thirteen persons, for thefts to the amount of sixty-one shillings and sixpence, received transportation to the amount of one hundred and twelve years; that in Wiltshire seventeen persons, for thefts to the value of four pounds and ninepence received transportation to the amount of one hundred and thirty-two years; and again in Sussex eight persons, for thefts to the aggregate amount of fourteen shillings and sixpence, received transportation to the amount of sixty-two years, or the very great judicial bargain of four years and five months of convict life for the small sum of one shilling. Taking four dozen cases out of this report, and reckoning them up; we find that twelve pounds nine shillings and a pennyworth of larceny got in exchange, three hundred and seventy-six years of transportation.

But we are still dealing in generalities. It is possible for a shilling to be stolen in a way that is more absolutely wicked than some other theft of fifty pounds. The robbers of the widow's mite[5] cannot be punished too severely. Down we come, therefore, to special cases; and, not to be partial, will quit the south, and travel north to Yorkshire for them, after we have turned a few more abstract facts out of the Abstract Report now in our hands. In Dorset, G.B. received ten years' transportation for a shilling, T.C. ten years'. In Wiltshire, W.N., convicted on two charges—one for stealing property worth

---

[4] 'Callipash and Callipee': callipash, a yellowish, jellylike, edible substance adhering to the upper shell of a turtle; callipee is a similar substance adhering to the lower shell.

[5] Mite: a small sum or a coin of little value.

Figure 1.1 Convict embarking for Botany Bay by Thomas Rowlandson, c.1800. Image courtesy of National Library of Australia: nla.pic-an5601547.

two shillings, and the other for property worth three—received seven years for the two shillings, and ten for the three; so that for five shillings he had seventeen years of the public hospitality.

Now we will take a special note or two, and observe what kind of larcenies they are which have brought down these thunderbolts from the Joves enthroned at Quarter Sessions. At the Spring Sessions for the East

Riding of Yorkshire last year, George Ingram was transported for ten years; he had stolen five pigeons. At the Midsummer Sessions of the same Riding, William Sanders was transported for ten years; finding a dead sheep, he had taken half of it. At the Norfolk Quarter Sessions for March eighteen hundred and fifty-three, William Flood was transported for ten years; he had stolen a faggot.[6] At the same Sessions James Whip was transported for ten years, as a man who had received a coat, knowing it to be stolen, upon the sole evidence of the thief himself, who was the means of bringing him to justice.

At the Liverpool Borough Sessions, James MacGovan affected a great bargain—the wares of justice were in this case in fact given away like so much bankrupt stock; he obtained ten years' transportation for the sum of threepence-halfpenny.

At the Norfolk Quarter Sessions, last Midsummer, John Landimore for three successive thefts of corn from the same owner, received three successive sentences, and was transported accordingly for the term of thirty years. At the Leicester Borough Sessions last June, William Barret got ten years for tenpence. On the part of the justices, if we regard them as the shop-keepers of law, this must be considered very reckless trading.

Then, too, it is not fair trading. The very same County Criminal Reports, out of which we can pick forty-eight persons who had stolen, in all, less than thirteen pounds, and were therefore transported for three hundred and seventy-six years, being on an average seven or eight years per man, supply us also with the cases of another set of forty-eight prisoners who had stolen thirty times as much, in all more than four hundred pounds, and whose aggregate punishment was the mere trifle of imprisonment for sixteen years, two months and three days, being on an average four or five months per man. All depends on the temper, or the stomach, or the greater or less degree of shallowness in the particular cousin Shallow who may, in each case, be the prevailing dignitary.

We will not confine ourselves to generalities in making these comparisons. Let us take, here again, some sample cases from the bushel

---

[6] Faggot: a bundle of sticks—used for fuel, torches, for fencing and filling of ditches, etc.

ready to our hand. At the Dorset Quarter Sessions one November, a man, for a robbery of eighty pounds, was sentenced to six months' imprisonment. At the same Sessions, for the same offence at Midsummer, another man was sentenced to be transported for fourteen years. J.D. was then sentenced to six weeks' imprisonment for stealing ten pounds; but, at the Epiphany Sessions, E.A., who stole ten pounds, was imprisoned for two years. At the Michaelmas[7] Sessions, R.F., for stealing property worth threepence, was sentenced to imprisonment for one day, and S.B., an old man of seventy, for a theft of the same magnitude, was sentenced to imprisonment for one year with hard labour.

At the Somerset Epiphany Sessions, eighteen hundred and forty-nine, W.H., for a three-halfpenny theft was imprisoned for six months; and, at the Michaelmas Adjourned Sessions, B.C. received precisely the same punishment for a robbery of thirty-seven pounds.

At the Epiphany Sessions for Hampshire, eighteen hundred and forty-nine, T.W. received, for twenty-three pounds, six months' imprisonment, when J.G. got seven years of transportation for a shilling. We could continue almost indefinitely these chronicles of the Shallow family. We stop because they are becoming tedious. It is right, however, before we turn to other and more sensible topics, to point out that the inequalities of punishment thus evident are not to be accounted for by any theory within the reach of ordinary logic. They have little, and generally nothing, to do with previous convictions or the merits of the cases. We will show this by one or two other samples for which we have only to dip our hands into the bag.

At the Sussex Sessions, Midsummer eighteen hundred and forty-nine, S.H. was convicted upon three several charges for stealing property to the value of about eight pounds. He was sentenced to three days' imprisonment; upon a fourth case, for robbery to the value of three pounds, being proved against him, he was sentenced to six months' imprisonment. But at the same Sessions, J.P. was sentenced for a theft of four shillings to one week's

---

[7] Michaelmas: informal name for 'The day of St Michael and All Angels', the feast day held on 29 September. It was a calendar marker for the end of summer and also when rents were due.

imprisonment, and, upon the proving of a second case against him—a theft of one pound, twelve and ninepence—was transported for seven years.

At the Norwich Assizes last July, John Brown, who had been previously convicted of felony, was indicted with three other persons on three separate charges for stealing wheat, the property of the same prosecutor. He was found guilty on each indictment and imprisoned for eighteen months. But at the Norfolk Quarter Sessions last June, John Landimore, before mentioned, who had never before been convicted, was indicted with three others for the same offence in precisely the same way, and was transported for thirty years.

We have quoted a sentence of ten years' transportation for the theft of a faggot. The thief had certainly been once before convicted. But at the Woodbridge Summer Sessions, Thomas Longford was proved to have stolen two faggots and to have been once before convicted, yet was only imprisoned for six months; and at the East Kent Midsummer Sessions Thomas Longford, who stole three faggots and had been twice before convicted, had only a sentence of twelve month's imprisonment.

At the Norwich City Sessions last July, Thomas Cudden, for stealing one pig, was imprisoned for twelve months; when at the same Sessions, six months before, Samuel Brighton, who stole seven pigs, had only been imprisoned nine months, though he had been previously convicted of house-breaking and there had been recorded against him sentence of death.

Two boys, sixteen years old, were sentenced at the last York Summer Assizes to transportation, one for fifteen and the other for twenty years, in punishment for a theft of six shillings and sixpence from the person. A month afterwards, at the Liverpool Assizes, L., D., B., P. and K. were found guilty of a serious burglary. L., D., B. and P. had been convicted previously for felonies. L. had been convicted before of burglary and suffered eighteen months' imprisonment; had also been convicted of felony on one other occasion, six times again as a reputed thief. D. had been twice before found guilty of felony, and several times summarily convicted. P. had been twice convicted of felony, and once transported for ten years; also seven times summarily convicted. Punishments were distributed among them, varying from twelve months' imprisonment to twelve years' transportation; but not one of them had such a bargain as that allowed to the two boys who got between them thirty-five years of transportation for a highway robbery of six-and sixpence.

It is not our matter that is now exhausted, but our patience. We must quit the Shallows. When we have found out how to paint lilies roses, we shall have learnt how to comment upon facts like these.

2
Chip: The Antecedents of Australia
Irwin

Transportation of criminals to Australia: the first penal settlement.
Volume: 8 Number: 199 Pages: 476–77
Date: January 14, 1854
Fee: 15 shillings for 1 Column.

Transportation of criminals to the American colonies having ceased from the commencement of the war of independence, the jails in England were soon overflowing with criminals and reeking with disease. The Government therefore determined, upon the favourable representations of Captain Cook, to form a penal settlement upon that portion of the eastern coast of New Holland that had been named by him New South Wales. There he had discovered Botany Bay, so named by Banks and Solander—the naturalists who had accompanied Cook—from the abundance and variety of its then unknown productions. A few miles to the northward of Botany Bay he had named a magnificent inlet of the ocean Port Jackson; which now forms the harbour of Sydney—in beauty and extent second only to that of Rio Janeiro.

No time was lost in carrying the new scheme into operation. Captain Phillip was selected to take charge of the expedition and to superintend the formation of the penal colony. He sailed from England in May, seventeen hundred and eighty-seven, and in January of the following year landed at Port Jackson with seven hundred and fifty-seven convicts.

From this small beginning have sprung, at various intervals, the colonies of Australia and Van Dieman's Land. It was only in eighteen hundred and thirty-five, that Governor Sir R. Bourke came down from Sydney with Mr. Lonsdale, the surveyor, and a few others, and laid out the plan of the town of

Melbourne on the banks of the Yarra Yarra. However, had it not been for this system of transportation, many more years must have elapsed before the capabilities of this extraordinary country could have become known. There were no visible inducements to attract towards it any private enterprise. It was not until the Government had, by the aid of the criminals, caused the country to be opened up, the fertility of its soil to be made known, and the suitableness of many of its districts for pastoral purposes to be quite understood, that emigration properly began. Sixty-three years ago, nothing but the existence of Australia was known—now it is a foremost figure in our picture of the History that has yet to be acted in the world.

3
Going Circuit at the Antipodes
Henry Morley and Archibald Michie

An insight into the legal system of NSW and its treatment of Aboriginal offenders.
Volume: 4 Number: 92 Pages: 344–48
Date: January 3, 1852
Fee: 4 pounds 4 shillings for 9 Columns.

Delightful is the morning when, after a tedious voyage, just as you begin to wonder where all the continents and islands in the world can be hidden, a lusty voice shouts 'Land ho!' from the mast-head. And there, as we see now from the deck, is a long wall of coast, which appears suddenly to have stepped out of a cloud! And there, too, is the lighthouse!

The ship's nose is immediately put in the right direction, and in about half-an-hour we descry a boat bobbing up and down in the swell of the sea. She is rowed by about half-a-dozen athletic, copper-coloured New Zealanders, and steered by a pleasant-looking pilot, seated in the stern-sheets. We have scarcely time to wonder why we think this pilot worthy of being taken to our hearts and embraced, before he springs on board, asks for the news, shakes hands with, and deposes, the captain, who retires into insignificance, whilst the New Zealanders, having made fast their boat to our stern, sit and criticise us at their leisure.

With the usual luffing[1] and shouting of 'tacks and sheets,' and the average driving about of the sailors, by the uncompromisingly despotic pilot, we find ourselves entering between the huge heads of Port Jackson. In about a

---

[1] Luffing: to bring the head of vessel near to the wind.

quarter of an hour more, we are safely out of the vast Pacific, and gliding along the serene and sparkling surface of Sydney harbour.

Picturesque and Claude-like as this scene is at all times, it is strikingly so when you enter it for the first time, after a four months' voyage. You appear to be sailing up a beautiful lake, delightfully variegated with islands dotted about upon its transparently blue water. On either side, little promontories jut out into the harbour, crowned by mansions, cottages, and windmills, all bright and glowing in the clear air; while the eye in vain endeavours to penetrate to the heads of all the pretty little bays which are formed by the irregularities of the shore. At all times, in favourable weather, the harbour is alive with boats which skim like sea-birds round a newly-arrived London ship. The harbour being completely land-locked and protected from all weathers, we sail out of a rough sea, into water almost as smooth as a mill-dam. So sudden is the change from rough to smooth, that we seem to have reached a charmed and silent region, where some good Prospero works his tranquillising spells. We are very soon, however, reduced from Shakespearean fancies to matters of fact, by the sounds of 'Want a boat, sir?' startling us in our reverie, like the ghost of a voice from the Thames.

We got—I and my wife—into the waterman's boat. The child-like and warm-hearted tars[2] give us three hearty cheers as we are pulled away from the ship's side; and, after about ten minutes' passage up the harbour, and into Sydney Cove, among shipping from all parts of the world, we pull up at the Queen's Wharf. We pay the waterman a shilling, astonished to find the nature and uses of that coin so distinctly understood at the Antipodes, and are once again on terra firma.

The early part of the day appeared to have been rainy in town, and the place was wet and puddled. The footpaths were merely paved in patches here and there, and three-story houses of bad-complexioned brick were huddled up, with wretched hovels of weatherboard, and occasionally vacant spaces, or dust heaps. Here and there, a dray,[3] or a mouldy-looking superannuated gig, behind an ungroomed horse, as dripping and dejected as if he were serving

---

[2] Tar: a sailor.
[3] Dray: a cart.

out a sentence of hard labour, were almost all the vehicles we met. The singular frequency, too, of the children of Israel—at times unpleasantly economical of soap—was not, upon the whole, more exhilarating than the prevalence of badly-cut slop apparel, in windows and at doors. A good part of Monmouth Street had apparently got the start of us, and had already settled down, squalidly well-off, as at home.

Public-houses were in good force, addressing themselves to the colonial thirst by the usual eye-catching announcements in long black letters, down the fronts of various tenements, that 'Guinness's XXX,' or 'Allsopp's Ale,' or 'London Particular,' might be had inside. The live part of the scene generally consisted of sailors, brokers, clerks, draymen, New Zealanders, one or two aboriginal blacks, and one or two score of goats and dogs. Upon the whole, we were very much astonished by our first impression; for we somewhat hastily adopted this quarter of the town as a fair sample of the whole. We concluded about as wisely and as justly as a Frenchman would, if he were suddenly to judge of London from a hasty glance at Wapping. Every large port must have a Wapping, and here was the Sydney Wapping; the only difference being, that it was a Wapping in its teens.

Taking our ease in our inn the first night—and what ease, after such a voyage!—we sallied out, in the bright delicious freshness of the following morning, to investigate the field of our future operations. I qualify my sketch with the results of a subsequent nine year's experience.

The habits and fashions of a people stick to them wherever they go. Algiers would probably now remind us of Paris, as Sydney certainly reminds us of many a sea-port town that we have seen in England. There is the same style of houses and shops, and plate-glass fronts. On all sides you see a bustling throng of merchants, tradesmen, clerks, porters, sea captains, operatives, farmers, and long-bearded squatters in tweeds. Men of business on horseback, and in every kind of carriage, from the most stylish phaeton,[4] to the rustiest of primeval gigs, pour from the picturesque suburbs into town after breakfast. Drays pass to and fro with all sorts of merchandise from ships. Other drays, in the wool season, are bringing in their bales of wool, for

---

[4] Phaeton: a type of light four-wheeled open carriage.

shipment to London. Omnibuses[5] rattle by. Rows of handsome hackney carriages—once private, but which insolvency of former owners has placed at the disposal of the public—occupy their respective stands; their drivers evincing the same taste for extortion as their English brethren. The butcher's boy calls for orders; the baker, enthroned on his cart, dispenses his bread with English punctuality. The 'vegetable man' takes his rounds with his pony cart (donkeys being almost unknown), and cries carrots and turnips as excruciatingly as in the old world. Fishmongers' shops there are none; supplies in this line being brought to the doors by men with barrows. One of these dealers well stocked with bream, snapper, whiting, flathead, &c., you may occasionally see (as you pass along the street,) chaffering with servant girls at the door-steps; and, upon the conclusion of the bargain, set about bleeding a lobster, as large—without any exaggeration—as a new-born baby.

In the after-part of the day, the town, of course, undergoes a change in the appearance of the wayfarers. Here, again, we tread closely upon the heels of the Londoners. Ladies in a Colony by no means lose their taste for shopping. From three to five o'clock, you may see plenty of neat boots and sandalled insteps twinkling across the pavement, every few yards, between shops and carriages, and carriages and shops; and that abominable speech, 'What is the next article, madam?' punishes husbands equally on both sides of the world. Gay officers, charming fellows, scatter fascination as they lounge along. In the evening you may go to the theatre and hear an opera—'Fra Diavolo,' 'Maritana,' or the 'Bohemian Girl'—performed as well as in any provincial theatre of the mother country. The Jews and the operatives, with a sprinkling of other classes, are the steadiest supporters of the drama. The aristocracy—don't smile! We *have* an aristocracy; how could Englishmen get on without one!—the aristocracy eschew the drama as vulgar, except when the Governor goes.

At midnight you leave the theatre. If intent upon devilled kidneys, native oysters, or any other established form of post-theatrical supper, you can be accommodated at a variety of good taverns, and at moderate rates. If you are a sensible man, you wend your way homewards, astonished, perhaps, to find

---

[5] Omnibus: a large horse-drawn carriage.

that this great felonious city of the South (as depicted by the Earl of Shaftesbury) is actually as quiet as a Scotch town in church time. And yet, lighted by gas as you go, you are walking on ground which, little more than sixty years ago, was a mere bush—nursery of kangaroos and opossums.

From this city, after the discovery of California, until within the last few months, people of the middle and working classes poured by thousands into the great American Dorado. And although our population—that is to say, the population of the town alone—had attained, before this curious migration commenced, to something near sixty thousand souls; and although George Street, Sydney, was nearly as long as Oxford Street, London; the colonists generally began to have serious fears about so heavy a drain upon a country, which, at the best of times, is but ill-supplied with labour. In due time, however, news arrived of Californian fever, Californian ague, Californian revolvering, and Californian potatoes at tenpence a pound; all which items of intelligence coming together, naturally abated the fever for moving. Again, however, it broke out, about twelve months ago; and, ship-load after ship-load of human beings, many of them far from poor, left Port Jackson for San Francisco—a two month's voyage. Now, New South Wales has opened a Dorado of her own, and the hungerers for wealth are running back from California to their old colony.

My own 'diggins' were in the Supreme Court. I had therefore, for some years, little travel in this interesting country, other than such as an attendance on the circuits imposed. These circuits are held twice a year; at Maitland, Goulburn, Moreton Bay, and Bathurst, the new gold field. One trip to Maitland will put you fully in possession of the travelling means and appliances, and the common life, of the colony at large.

My first Maitland trip was made under auspices very favourable to my acquiring knowledge of the state of the country. A fellow-counsel had invited myself, my wife, and child, to spend a few days with him at his place on the Hunter, on our way to the assize town,[6] and we all started together.

By train? No; towards that sort of thing we only turned the first turf a few months ago; and if you had only heard all the fine things said on that

---

[6] Assize town: a circuit court.

occasion, you would have been astonished at the modesty of Britons. At ten o'clock, P.M., the two counsels, each with a wife and child, left their houses for the Hunter River Steam Navigation Company's wharf, situated on that branch of the magnificent Port Jackson, called Darling Harbour.

Coaches, cabs, drays, trucks, and highly-excited porters were making an astounding din. The storm of goods, packages, and parcels of all kinds for the Hunter—Sydney being the heart through which all manufactured supplies are passed into the Hunter River district—gave a very strong Thames Street expression to the scene. Through this Babel we gained the deck of the beautiful boat, the 'Rose;' the bell rang; we ran down the harbour, and in half-an-hour were pitching (as we passed through the heads) on the heavy ground swell of the great Pacific. I could not pass through that mighty gap in the iron-bound coast, without a sort of admiring wonder at the vast strides which Englishmen had made in this part of the world, since Cook, in his good ship 'Endeavour,' first sighted, some sixty years since, the strange land. Here were we quite at home in a first-rate English-built steamer: her swift wheels grasping the great seas, and throwing them contemptuously behind her as she flew onward upon her course. Here were London barristers going circuit on the South Pacific! I thought of man's triumphs over the deep, until I distinctly felt the deep triumphing over me—whereupon I went below.

The cabin was, and is (for the beautiful 'Rose' still runs), large and well lighted; along two tiers of shelves, on which the beds were made, reclined all the male passengers in layers, and one over the other, like bodies in a family vault. Here, we lay for the next five or six hours. No human sound mixed itself with the incessant creaking and thrashing of the ocean by our paddles, except an occasional faint and plaintive cry of 'Steward!' Thus we all remained until dawn, when the mate cried down the stairs, 'Any one for Newcastle?'

We went up. We found we were near the great Breakwater being formed by convicts: a yellow and brown parti-coloured[7] swarm of whom were watching us as we rounded 'Nobby's,' a high rock. This Breakwater, since finished, makes Newcastle a safe and excellent port, in which vessels of any

---

[7] Parti-coloured: variegated, having different colours in different parts.

tonnage may lie in any wind. In a few minutes we passed once again into smooth water (after a night run of eight hours along the coast), and presently were alongside the wharf at Newcastle, a dull, dingy, coal-producing spot. Here, staying an hour, we took in fuel, and then steamed for the mouth of the Hunter, near which Newcastle is situated. The banks of this river were low, flat, and uninteresting. Between clumps of dwarf mango-trees, I could just catch glimpses of what seemed yellow enough to be a bit of the Great Desert; and in this part, small groups of cattle appeared to be engaged in a severe search for grass. I learned that this yellow-looking vegetation was a kind of marshy reed, of which cattle are passionately fond. In about an hour—the river being for the whole distance about as broad as the Thames at Westminster—we arrived at our destination, the vessel ran up to Walker's wharf, and we landed at once upon his property.

A long and winding road, cut through the forest of gum-trees, conducted us to his then temporary house. Having breakfasted, we sallied forth to look at the property. Along the river-side, varying in depth inland, the soil is commonly very rich, as is usually the case on the banks of Australian rivers. Here, were settled, some in slab huts, others in cottages of rather better description, about twenty or thirty tenants renting small portions of land on clearing leases; the little homesteads being visible from the steamer, as she passed up or down the river. I visited these cottages, inspected the little farms, talked with the tenants (who were glad to find an attentive listener to their narratives of early difficulties conquered by perseverance), and found that all but one had been the very poorest bounty emigrants from England and Ireland. They did not disguise that they had flown from little better than starvation in their own country. Each tenant had small patches of Indian corn, wheat, barley, potatoes, and tobacco, besides a very well-stocked kitchen-garden. Some few had a cow, most of them possessed pigs, and all were overrun with abundance of poultry of every kind. The virgin soil gave them two crops a year of everything, for a mere scratching on the surface. All mere animal wants were supplied in abundance, and some few had books.˜

There was a school, but no church nearer than Raymond Terrace, distance some seven or eight miles. In the course of our long walk this day, we stumbled across a king. Kings[8] are by no means uncommon in this country. I have had a king and two or three black princes, all warming themselves together upon a dust-heap in my back-yard in Sydney. Walker's present king was as black as a coal: limited in respect of apparel, and, to the best of my nose, not happy in the royal perfumer. Round his neck, hanging by a string, was a brass plate (like a waterman's badge), with his name and rank, King Toocooioo, engraved on it. This plate, of which he was as proud (and why not?) as if it were a blue ribbon or a garter, had been originally given to him by some settler, and it was always worn as a badge of dignity among his tribe. The king was easy in his manners, lithe as a panther in his movements, and allowed no false delicacy to stand between him and his royal comfort. After obtaining Walker's leave to call upon his kitchen, he demanded of him (pointing deliberately at me), 'Who dis swell, Sar?' Now, as I was dressed in plain black, I was a little disconcerted at this frank and sincere description of my personal appearance, and was at first inclined to think that our black friend thought every man a dandy who was effeminate enough to wear a pair of pantaloons. I afterwards learned that the blacks, in acquiring our language, have seldom had any other masters than the assigned convict-servants of the settlers, and that the word 'swell' is used as seriously as we use the word 'gentleman.'

This king had left his subjects, or, rather, his companions (for they paid him neither respect nor taxes), a few miles up the river, at the Government township, called Raymond Terrace; and upon hearing of the arrival of Mr. and Mrs. Walker, his majesty had hastened down to pay his respects, and establish himself comfortably about the premises.

The king, always, summer and winter, slept in the open air; and, so far, was right royal enough in his exemption from rent and taxes. Lords of the bed-chamber were wanting, it is true; and what was perhaps of still more importance, blankets and sheets. I had a great desire to see his majesty in bed—if such an expression may be used—and, at about nine o'clock in the evening, I prevailed upon Walker to go forth with me, from his own cheerful fire-side, to beat up the black king's quarters.

---

[8] Kings: Aboriginal elders/leaders.

The night was dark, and, for New South Wales, cold. We took a plate full of honeycomb with us as a present to His Majesty. About three or four hundred yards off in the forest, and within forty or fifty yards of one of the white men's huts, we saw and heard the black man's fire crackling and blazing cheerily, and lighting up the sides of the trees and of the hut with a rich glare. Strange, and passing melancholy sight, this startling contrast between civilised and savage life. Under that cottage roof was reposing a snug family of whites, tucked in amongst sheeting and British blankets; and there, only a few yards off, in the star-light night, is a black brother, whose only lodging is 'on the cold ground.' The white peasant, it is to be hoped, says his prayers; the black king, it is to be feared, has no sense, or if any, the most vague sense, of religion or of Deity.

As we approached, I was a little surprised that no living figure could be seen near the fire. 'Oh!' said Walker, 'he is gone perhaps to try to get an opossum for his supper.' We had approached within two or three yards of the fire, without discovering our friend, and I had concluded that he was away somewhere in the woods, when suddenly I started as I saw what at first looked like a huge black maggot wriggling about under a very rude structure of boughs, placed against the wind, and on the other side of the fire. A second glance showed me the king. Completely unrobed, he was rolling about in ecstasies of warmth. He looked like an animal roasting itself alive, and liking it. We presented our honey-comb, which he ate (wax and all), and when done, he again abandoned himself to his repose, without thanking us, or bidding us good night, or asking us to take anything—except the plate, after he had cleaned it carefully with his forefinger.

After a stay of seven or eight days, Walker and myself, leaving our wives behind, mounted a pair of his horses for the purpose of proceeding through the Bush to Maitland, where the causes[9] were to be tried by the then Chief Justice (since dead); and with the trifling colonial incident of passing a night

---

[9] Causes: any suit or action in court.

Figure 1.2 Neddy Noora Shoalhaven, Shoalhaven tribes by Charles Rodius, 1834. Image courtesy of Mitchell Library, State Library of New South Wales: PXA 615 NO.11.

in a slab hut, we arrived at Maitland, by ten o'clock next morning. We pricked our steeds into the hotel, not unworthy of old England; and after a hearty breakfast at the bar mess, donned our wigs and gowns for action. Our Chief Justice had a charge prepared, and we were all expected to attend and hear it.

As soon as this preachment, and the proclamation against vice and profaneness, had duly provoked the wit of the bystanders, the Solicitor-General required two blacks to be put to the bar, charged with spearing cattle, the property of a settler. The names in which these sable offenders rejoiced, were Wellington and Fryingpan; playful appellatives, originally conferred upon them by some of the convict-servants of neighbouring settlers. For some reason, which I now forget, Fryingpan was not tried, but Wellington was duly brought up. He was a tall gaunt fellow, apparently about thirty-five years old (but probably much younger, as these blacks soon age in appearance), with large, flashing, expressive, deep-set eyes. A dirty blanket was his only covering; a huge mop of coarse matted black hair, hung about his shoulders; and he had mouth enough for two faces. He was led in by the Chief Constable, and, as it was obviously his first appearance upon that stage, he was by no means perfect in the part of a prisoner. He required considerable shoving and pulling to get him into a sort of bin, called the dock; and probably if he had been left to himself, he would have selected a seat beside the judge.

When fairly confronted with Sir James, a violent grin broke out half round Wellington's head, evidently caused by his Honour's wig, bands, and red gown, on which the savage's eyes seemed to be fastened with a fascinated stare. Nor did he, in his unsophisticated nature, attempt to conceal the emotion excited within him; for, notwithstanding the additional gravity laid on by the judge for the occasion, the joke appeared to improve so much in the black man's mind, that at last he laughed outright. Moreover he seemed to grin a kind of circular invitation to all the people in Court to join in the laugh with him. He grinned the rebukeful countenance of the Sheriff into such a state, that that solemn officer of Justice was obliged abruptly to turn his face away, and discharge a short private laugh of his own. He grinned at the counsel and the crowd, until giggling became irrepressible, and even the countenance of the Chief Justice, who had a keen perception of the ludicrous, was becoming rapidly unmanageable.

As soon as this general break-out had been duly snubbed and got under, it became necessary to appoint an interpreter to act between the prisoner and the crown, as the prisoner was utterly ignorant of English. A white man who understood, or professed to understand, Wellington's particular dialect, was in Court, and being sworn duly to interpret, the information (in England, the indictment) was read and translated to the prisoner. The Chief Justice, looking as unconscious as he could of the fact that Wellington was still half swooning with delight, called upon him, through the interpreter, to plead to the information. The interpreter having translated and apparently explained it, a short, voluble, and eager conversation of some minutes ensued, before the black appeared to comprehend what was required of him. At last he mastered it, and promptly delivering his answer, the interpreter proceeded with respectful gravity to communicate it to the Court. 'May it please your honour, he only says it's all a pack of lies, and that *he* never speared the cattle at all; but he thinks he knows the black fellow that did spear them, and he will bring him down to the Court in a few days, if your honour will allow him to go and look for him.' This is a style of defence as popular among the blacks as an *alibi* may be in England. Wellington, however, was contradicted by several witnesses who took him in the fact, and therefore he was found guilty, and sentenced to transportation for ten years to Van Diemen's Land. He was removed from the bar, looking as if he had got to the end of a pleasant entertainment, and as if the memory of the Chief Justice's wig would be a solace to him in his saddest hours.

Being at this time young to the country, I felt for this cheerful Wellington. What right have we, thought I, to seize this poor child of nature, haul him into an English court of justice, mock his ignorance with a jargon of law forms, and conclude by tearing him from his hunting grounds, his wife, and little children, for ten years? How complacently we look upon his savage ignorance! and for certain he is ignorant enough; but how far are we removed from the same charge, when, by elaborate forms, and upon assumptions of his moral and legal responsibility, we try a creature who has about as clear an understanding of the whole proceeding as a dog? Yet, what else is to be done? Must not property of colonists be protected? And how may this be, unless the blacks be made amenable to the law? To shoot them, would be plain unvarnished murder,—which, however, has been extensively committed before now,—and their aggressions, unresisted, would soon swamp the colony. The colonists, therefore, become reconciled to the prosecutions of the blacks. If they cannot understand law, they understand punishment.

Nothing of criminal interest, beyond the above-described trial, took place at these assizes. We wound up, of course, as usual, with a dinner given to the judge by the townspeople and settlers. About a hundred white waistcoats, and an almost infinite variety of badly cut coats, sat down to a table as well covered, and in a room as well furnished, as you could meet with in old England—always kept by colonists before them for a pattern. Toasts, compliments, speech-making, and all the usual dreariness, prevailed until ten o'clock, at which hour I withdrew to bed. I tried to be deaf to the jingling of the glasses, to the hammering of the table, to the cheers, and the comic songs, and the wild roars of laughter, which increased towards midnight amongst the diners; most of whom were farmers and gentlemen-settlers of unlimited powers of digestion, and incredulous of headaches. Once or twice, indeed, as the laughter became almost too exciting for my curiosity, I could almost have got out of bed, and returned to the table in my night-gown, to request that that last 'good thing' might be repeated. Gradually, I fell asleep to this wild accompaniment; perhaps fancying myself wiser, and more temperate than the hearty revellers; whereas, I was only more dyspeptic.

4
Convicts in the Gold Region
Richard H. Horne

Penal stockades and prison ships in Melbourne.
Volume: 8 Number: 182 Pages: 49–54
Date: September 17, 1853
Fee: 5 pounds 5 shillings for 10 Columns.

On arriving at the main Sydney route from the town boundary of
Melbourne—Melbourne famous, among other things, ever since it rose to
fame two years ago, for no roads, or the worst roads, or impassable sloughs,
swamps, and rights of way through suburb wastes of bush, and boulder
stones, and stumps of trees—leaving, I say, all these peculiarities behind, you
suddenly arrive at the opening of the main road to Sydney, leading in a direct
line to the village of Pentridge, the position of the Convict Stockade. This is
the chief penal depôt of the colony.

The first thing that strikes you, after all you have gone through, is the
excellence of the road, its directness, and its length. You look along a straight
road, broad, well-formed, hard, clean, with drains running along each side,
protected (together with the lower edges of the road) by large boulder-stones
and heavy logs at intervals, and the eye traverses along this to an unvarying
distance of two miles and a quarter. There is no road to be compared with it
in the colony, and the whole of this has been the product of convict labour,
within the space of little more than two years and four or five months. Be it
understood very great difficulties had to be overcome, in respect of swamps,
huge stones, and large trees, and stumps with great roots. Nor was this the
whole of the work performed by the convicts of Pentridge, a bridge and part
of a road elsewhere having been constructed simultaneously; the bridge

alone, if it had been built by free labour during these periods of high wages, being of the value of five thousand pounds. Whatever the saving as to cost, however, the value of a good road and a bridge to a new country like this is almost beyond calculation. I forget what practical philosopher it was who said, 'The worst use you can put a man to is to hang him,' but surely most people will readily admit that such a road as the above, in any country, and more especially in the colony of Victoria, is not only far more useful, but a far more humane and sightly object than the gallows.

The road to Pentridge gradually and slightly rises till you reach the top, when a turn to the right brings you at once upon the ground of the Stockade, which lies in a hollow a little below. A first impression does not convey any adequate impression of its strength, or general character as a penal establishment. You see several detached tents upon the higher ground, with a sentinel walking to and fro in front of them; and you look down upon a low-roofed, straggling range of buildings, something in appearance between an English country brewhouse, and a military outpost holding it in charge. Descending the slope, and reaching the house of the superintendent, a square garden of cabbages, and square beds of weeds mixed with flowers and shrubs (a type of most of the gardens since the discovery of the gold), is seen on the other side of the horse-way between, with a green swampy field beyond, bounded by a long iron-grey wall of large loose stones, with a few trees to the right, and the head of a sentinel moving backwards and forwards—upon legs we assume—in the meadow or marsh below on the other side.

Being left alone for a while under the wooden verandah of the house, the picture is further enlivened by the slow approach of a cow from a cow-house in the proximity of the cabbage square, which pauses and looks at me with a rueful and rather commiserating expression. She is pretty comfortable herself, but she sees that I am a new comer, and wonders perhaps what I have done to be brought there. The place is all very silent; so is the cow; so of course am I. A dog now comes round the corner, and after looking at me, without barking or other demonstration, retires. I follow mechanically, and on turning the angle of the house I come in view of what I had at first compared in my mind to a country brewhouse, which on a closer examination becomes formidable enough, presenting as it does very unmistakeable indications of strength, precaution, and watchful vigilance, both within and without. No voice is heard; nothing is heard but the clash of the chains of a gang of convicts passing across one of the yards.

The Superintendent, Mr. Barrow, who is at the head of the penal establishments of the colony, appears, and on my making some allusion to the men in chains, gives me their collective history in a few words, which show that the said chains are by no means unnecessary ornaments. Most of the convicts have been, in one place or other, prisoners from childhood. They have been three times convicted at home; first of all, whipped, perhaps, in the Parkhurst prison for juvenile offenders. After being exposed to the contaminating influence of many more depraved than themselves they have been pardoned, and sent adrift on the world, worse than when they entered it. Again apprehended and convicted they have been sent to Pentonville, or some other prison. Liberated after years, again following a course of crime, and once more apprehended and convicted, they have been transported to Van Diemen's Land, or Norfolk Island. At each of these places, and in all their prisons, at home and abroad, the pet system of penal training and reform in use at the period has been tried, and all have failed. Obtaining their conditional pardons, after a certain number of years in Van Diemen's Land, or Norfolk Island, they have had it in their power to go with their ticket of leave to any of the Australian colonies. Of course they have made directly for Melbourne—first to the gold region of the diggings, and next to the more fixed gold region of the wealthy community in the town. Most of the crimes of these men—that is to say, ninety per cent. of them, have originated in England. They had their chief experience and training at home. They have committed every crime here, to obtain gold, which their previous knowledge, skill, and depravity could suggest—and here they are at last.

It is night; a cold wind blows and a drizzling rain falls. An iron tongue, that is to say, a large bell in the Stockade, now announces that the time has arrived for all the prisoners to go to bed. A jingling of chains is heard as the several gangs pass across the yard, then a sound of the drawing of bolts, then silence. I cannot help speculating on the different sorts of suppressed ferocity in the faces of all these subdued human tigers, as they sit up on their wooden pallets, or look out from beneath their blankets.

Dining with the Superintendent, and the chief officer in command of this department (an old army captain), we are waited upon by one of the Aborigines, whose black face is without a single tint of negro brown. He is a prisoner of the Stockade, but in reward for a long period of good conduct, is entrusted with this comparative degree of liberty. He understands enough English—chiefly nouns, with a few morsels of verbs—to wait [on tables] very well; and though in his training he let fall or otherwise demolished a fearful amount of plates, glasses, and other strange and wondrous domestic articles which were previously unknown to his hands or eyes, he has now attained sufficient skill to avoid all such disasters. But he has his many old misfortunes of this kind in constant memory, and is full of dreadful apprehensions at every feat he performs. When he places a decanter of wine on the table, he remains a second or two with glaring eyes, and slowly withdrawing his open hands from both sides, ready to catch it in case it should take a fit of tumbling over as he walks away. He has an awful look of care in handing me a large dish of smoking potatoes. It seems like a solemn rite to an idol. I do not dare to glance up at his face. His constant care and watchfulness are extraordinary, and he obviously possesses far more intelligence than the Aborigines of Australia are generally believed capable of acquiring. Mr. Barrow informs me that he is really in all ordinary respects a very good and trusty servant, and that he has never been known to tell an untruth.

But the picture I have formed in my imagination, of all those fierce convicts in their chains—which are not taken off even at night—sitting up in their dens, or scowling up from beneath their blankets, still haunting me, I feel obliged to communicate my wish to Mr. Barrow to be permitted, if not contrary to rules, to pay them a passing visit forthwith. My wish being courteously accorded, I accompany the captain to the gate of the Stockade, and having passed this, and the armed sentinels, I find myself in a sort of barrack-yard, to appearance, with store-rooms at each side, having strong narrow doors, immense iron bolts, and an iron grating above for ventilation. The captain informs me that the stores are not thus protected to prevent anybody from walking off with them, but to render it almost impossible for the stores themselves to escape. These strong rooms are, in fact, the wards, or dormitories of the convicts.¯

Being invited to look in upon them, I approach one of these bolted doors. A square shutter is unfastened and pushed aside by the captain, and displays an iron grating through which I look at the irreclaimables in their lairs. How absurdly different is the reality from the picture I had framed in my imagination! Over a large room are distributed on stretchers, or other raised surface, and all so close together as only to allow of space for passage round each, a number of bundles of bedding, apparently, each enveloped in a grey and blue chequered coverlid of the same pattern. The bales or bundles are without motion or sound; no voice is heard, no head or foot is visible. Each bundle contains the huddled up form of a convict, who adopts this plan to obtain the greatest degree of warmth. Some are, no doubt, asleep; many wide awake, and full of peculiar thoughts: and perhaps even of fresh plans, should they ever again get a chance. What a volume of depraved life, what a prison-history lies enfolded in each of those moveless coverlids! There is absolutely nothing more to be seen, and we pass on to the next door. It is very much the same.

A third ward, however, presents a difference, the sleeping places being built up in separate berths, formed of cross battens, like very strong wooden cages for bears. The occupants of the upper tier ascend by means of a wooden bracket which juts out about half way up. Here I did see one foot protruding, belonging probably to some tall man who was not in irons. A lanthorn[1] is suspended from the centre of the roof, by a cord which is passed over a pulley, and runs through a hole above the door, so that the guard can raise it or lower it at any time during the night without opening the door. When the light needs trimming, the lanthorn being lowered, one of the prisoners, whose turn it is, has to get up and attend to it. The gleam it sheds is very melancholy, almost funereal. Hard natures, indeed, must they be, who, lying awake sometimes in the night, are not softened to a few serious thoughts or emotions as they look around them; but hard no doubt they are, and most of them of the hardest.

---

[1] Lanthorn: a lantern.

The Superintendent has work to do in his office—letters, reports, calculations, accounts, &c.; he becomes absent and taciturn, and I betake myself to bed. Throughout the whole night, I am awakened every half hour by the Stockade bell, and am five times informed, by the different voices of five sentinels, heard in succession from different points of the building, near and remote, that 'all's well!' After the sixth or seventh round of this, however, I get used to it, and drop to sleep again after hearing the satisfactory announcement.

Figure 1.3 Prison hulk, Hobsons Bay by David M. Little, c.1853. Image courtesy of La Trobe Picture Collection: State Library of Victoria.

Early in the morning, Billy—the Aboriginal—comes bolt into my room with my boots in one hand, and a jug of hot water in the other. He neither utters a word, nor looks at me (except in a way he has with his eyeballs turned *from* me), but places the boots on the floor, hovering with one hand over them in case either of them should fall sideways, and then sets the jug upon the dressing-table. He stares at it with a warning, or rather a threatening, look, when, seeing that it stands firmly, his gloomy features relax, and he departs as abruptly as he entered.

At seven o'clock the bell calls the convicts to a general muster in the principal yard, preparatory to the different gangs being marched off to their various descriptions of work. Mr. Barrow accompanies me into the yard. We pass through the little narrow massive gate, and I am at once in the presence of the thrice picked and sifted incorrigibles of the mother country and her Australian colonies. Sentinels, with loaded muskets, patrol the outskirts of the yard, and officers and constables armed with truncheons stand on guard outside the ranks. Many of the convicts have irons on their legs, but the majority are quite free, and can 'make a rush' if they will.

The convicts are ranged like a regiment of soldiers at muster, the rear ranks taking open order. They are all dressed in the usual grey, or dark pepper-and-salt coarse cloth. The yard is quite silent, and the names are called over. None of the black sheep are missing. I look along the ranks from face to face—with apparent indifference, casually, and with as little offence or purpose in my gaze as possible; and I am quite sure that it is not from knowing what they are, but really from a genuine impression of what is written by the fingers of experience in very marked lines and characters, and fluctuating or fixed shades, that I am persuaded there is not one good face among them. No, not one. On the contrary, nearly every face is extremely bad. I go over them all again in the same casual, purposeless way (they are not deceived by it a bit), and I feel satisfied that a worse set of fellows never stood in a row than those before me. Beneath that silent outwardly subdued air there is the manifest lurking of fierce, depraved, remorseless spirits, ready with the first chance to rush away into the course of crime that brought them here. By this time they are all at work upon me, quietly speculating on who I am, what I want, and if my visit portends anything to them. The yard is covered with loose stones of broken granite; and I notice close to my feet, and looking up directly into my face, a magpie. He also, holding his head on one side interrogatively, seems to ask my business here. I take a fresh breath as I look down at the little thing, as the only relief to the oppressive sense of prison doom that pervades the heavy scene.

The different working gangs are now marched off, about twenty at a time, with a sufficient interval both of time and distance between each, in case of a combination for a rush. Some go to work at building, some on the roads, some to the bridges, some to shoe-making, carpentering, &c. Tramp—tramp—tramp—with a jingle of irons—and they are all gone, and the little, narrow, massive gate is closed. The yard is vacant and silent, with nothing to be seen but the magpie hopping over the broken granite, and nothing now to be heard but the faint retiring jingle of the chains, the low continuous quire[2] of the frogs in the swamp, and the distant lowing of a forlorn cow.

It will have been evident before this, that everything is conducted here on a fixed system, rigidly and undeviatingly enforced, and that this is perfectly necessary, considering the subjects that have to be dealt with. No loud voice of command is ever heard, and the Superintendent has strictly forbidden all strong language on the part of the various officers and constables; the convicts are all controlled by the Stockade bell. When the bell orders them to come forth, they come forth; when the bell orders them to retire, they retire; if they are talking after retiring to rest, and the bell rings for silence, they are heard no more. Thus, all sense of personal tyrannies, and all special animosities, are avoided; the convicts feel they are under the spell of a sort of iron fate, a doom with an iron tongue—they are subdued and surrounded by an ever-vigilant and inflexible system, and they submit in spite of their will not to submit.

Mr. Barrow has been engaged in this anxious, painful, and unresting work these twelve long years—first in Norfolk Island, then in Van Diemen's Land, finally placed over Pentridge Stockade, the head-quarters of all the penal establishments of the colony. Of all public officers, there is probably not one whose duties are so full of sleepless anxieties, and so imperfectly appreciated (partly because they are but little known), as those he performs with such rigid constancy.

I have taken a stroll round the outskirts of the Stockade, and, while gazing over the swampy fields, now wearing the green tints of the fresh grass of winter which is near at hand, and thence turning my gaze to the bush in

---

[2] Quire: a choir.

the distance, with its uncouth and lonely appearance, I hear the jingle of chains to the left of where I am standing, and presently I see winding round the road a gang of convicts on their way to work at a bridge. They are succeeded by another gang; and, at the same interval, by a third. I am instantly and forcibly reminded of the string of convicts whom Don Quixote met and set at liberty, driving away their guards, taking off their fetters, and making them a noble speech; in return for which they ran off scoffing and hooting, and saluting their deliverer with a volley of stones. I never before felt so strongly the truthfulness of this scene. Here are a set of men who would have done—and who would this very day do—the same thing to any eccentric philanthropist in a broad-brimmed hat who should set them free and make them an address on liberty and humanity. So true may fiction be in the hands of genius.

Other convict establishments have been alluded to, which consist of two smaller stockades, and the hulks[3] which are lying in Hobson's Bay. The stockades being conducted in the same manner as the one just described, it will be unnecessary to particularize them, but I at once accept Mr. Barrow's obliging offer to take me on board the prison ships. We mount his gig and drive off.

On the way to Melbourne, through the bush, I ask many questions of the Superintendent—as to the growth of corn and cabbages—the latter, with other vegetables, being expensive luxuries in Melbourne. I also ask if the convicts can be trusted with edge tools, out of sight of the guards, or in sight? Is a funeral of one of them at all a melancholy sight to the others? and so forth. To these questions, I only receive monosyllabic replies, and often no reply; I half expect to get an answer from the distant bell. The Superintendent scarcely hears me; his mind is away at Pentridge, or on board one of his hulks. We pass through Melbourne, cross the bridge, and make our

---

[3] Prison hulks: when gold was found in Victoria, ex-convicts from neighbouring colonies rushed to the goldfields. The incidence of crime, chiefly robberies, rose to the point that prisons and stockades were soon full. As a result, prison hulks were established. Five ships were fitted out, as well as a guard ship to house the police. They were permanently moored in Hobson's Bay.

way along the muddy road to Liardet's Beach. I am indiscreet enough to ask a few more questions, but the anxious and absorbed look of the Superintendent shows me that he is absent from the gig, drive as well as he may, and I give it up. We arrive at the beach, and put off in the Government boat.

It is a long pull, and by no means a very lively one, for it is pretty clear that everybody in the boat feels a certain sort of cloud over his spirits from the serious business all are upon; but the sky is clear and bright, and I am soon in quite as absent a state as my friend the Superintendent, though it is probable that our thoughts are not in the same direction.

We first pull on board a hulk, a new one, to meet the rapidly increasing exigencies of the gold fields, which is being 'fitted up' as a convict ship. From the magnitude and strength of the wooden bars, rails, and battens, one might imagine that it was intended for young elephants, buffaloes, and wild boars. But I am assured by one of the wardens that they are not at all too strong. From this we row away to the prison ship for sailors—not convicts, but refractory. This word refractory includes all the offences of running away to the gold fields on the very first chance after the vessel drops her anchor in the bay, or of refusing their duty, or otherwise misconducting themselves while on board, with a view to distracting and overthrowing all arrangements for a most difficult port, and escaping in the confusion. To this hulk many captains of vessels have been obliged to send half their crews as soon as they have entered the harbour, and several have even adopted the more resolute plan of sending the whole crew off to prison at once, on the first show of insubordination, and keeping them there.

From the refractory, would-be gold-digging sailors' prison we push off for William's Town, and land near the light-house, at a little boat-pier of loose stones now in course of erection by a gang of convicts sent ashore for the purpose. Guards with loaded muskets patrol on the outskirts. It is a most useful work, and the extremity towards the water being made circular, for a small saluting battery, may serve to salute in another way, if there should ever be need. We pass from the pier to other works of building, drainage, and so on, all performed by convict labour: Mr. Barrow attending to his duties, and leaving me to stroll about and observe what I may, and judge for myself. To sum up all this in two words, I cannot perceive that the convicts have one spark of manly shame at their position; but I do most certainly observe that, without any hard words from the overseers, or the least personal violence (which would not for a moment be allowed), they do twice as much work in an hour as double the number of free Government labourers get through in a day. The chief reason seems to me to be that the convicts are thinking of their work as an agreeable relief after solitary confinement, and are glad to use their limbs; whereas the free labourers are thinking of the gold fields, and how to get ten shillings a day for doing nothing, until they are able to be off to the diggings.

The Superintendent now rejoins me, and carrying me along with him at a brisk pace, informs me that we are going on board the President, his principal convict hulk. This prison-ship contains the worst of the worst—men who cannot be trusted to work at anything—who pass their time in solitary confinement and in irons, excepting an hour's exercise on deck, when they are also handcuffed together—men for whom the Stockade of Pentridge is not an adequate protection—'the *crème de la crème,*' Mr. Barrow says, 'of the prisons of the mother country and her Australian colonies.'

We ascend to the deck, where the vessel, a little in front of the gangway, is separated by massive iron bars of some ten or eleven feet high from the rest of the ship. The Superintendent leaves me, as before, to attend to his duties of inspection, &c., but the chief officer in command (whose name I am rather uncomfortably startled at finding to be the same as my own) places me in charge of one of the head wardens, to accompany me where I wish to go. Of course I at once express a desire to pass through the great iron bars of this terrible cage, and to go below and see the *crème de la crème.*

We enter, and descend the ladder to the main deck. There is very little to be seen of a kind to make a picture, or a bit of description—in fact, nothing—all is in a state of severe, quiet, orderly, massive simplicity. The main deck is reduced to a passage, with rows of cells of immense strength on each side. The name of the occupant of the cell is written on a placard outside—with his crime, and the number of years for which he is sentenced. The great majority of offences are robbery with violence, and the term of imprisonment varies from five to twenty years. As I read I cannot say I at all envy the snug berth of my namesake in command. I feel that I would far rather be the Wandering Jew, or the captain of the Flying Dutchman. The cells are very like clean dens for wild beasts—their huge solid timbers and ironwork being quite strong enough for lions and tigers, bears and rhinoceroses, but not more so than necessary—so strong, so wilful, so resolute, and so unconquerable is man in his last stage of depravity. I express a desire to have the door opened of a certain cell, where the placard outside exercises a grim attraction upon me; but the warden at my side informs me that the convicts here are all under prolonged punishment, and my namesake does not consider it right to make a show of them. 'Oh, indeed,' I say—'very proper.'—'Not,' adds the warden, 'that it would hurt their feelings in any way; they are always too glad of any opportunity of having the door opened. We do not open it even at meal times; we push their allowance through a trap with a slide, which is instantly closed again and bolted.'—What a life for all parties!

I hear some of the prisoners singing in a low voice, and others holding a conversation between their partitions of four or five inches thick. To avoid some of the mental evils of long solitary confinement, they are wisely and humanely permitted to do this, provided no noise is made, or any loud tones audible. In an equally wise spirit Mr. Barrow has arranged a kind of prospect of amelioration; a degree of hope, well founded, however remote, is open to all. A certain number of years of good conduct here, gives the vilest ruffian of former times a fair prospect of removal to one of the Stockades; a certain number of years of good conduct there, gives him the probability of further promotion: namely, to work at some trade, or to go at large as a house servant and to attend in the yards; while, as a final result of many years of good conduct, he gets his ticket of leave to go where he pleases in the colony. Many do really reform, and lead decent lives thence-forth; some rush away to the gold fields—not to dig, but to plunder—and are back again heavily ironed, on board this dreadful prison-ship, in less than three months. The fresh term of punishment in these final of all final cases is twenty, or even thirty years. I inquire if they sink into utter hopeless despondency in such cases. 'No; only for the first week or two. After that they are again scheming, and plotting, and looking forward to some chance of escape.'

I hear a regular tramp going round overhead, accompanied by a jingling of chains. The warden informs me that ten of the convicts are now on deck for an hour's exercise. Only ten at a time are ever allowed to be out of their cells, none of these being ever trusted to go ashore to work, or to work at anything on board. I immediately go upon deck to have one look at the Superintendent's *crème de la crème*.

The ten men are all attired in the pepper-and-salt convict dress, with irons on their legs, and handcuffed together, two and two, as they walk round and round the main hatchway. I make no pretence of not looking at them; and they make none as to me. There is nothing violent or ferocious in the appearance of any of them; the predominating impression they convey is that of brutal ignorance, grossness, and utter absence of the sense of shame. The one who has most sense in his countenance is a dark, quiet, determined, patient villain, equal to any atrocity or daring. His look, as he comes round and faces me, never changes; most of the rest have some slight fluctuations. Presently they begin to whisper each other; and one makes a remark and passes it on; and presently they begin to exchange jokes, and indulge in a high degree of noiseless merriment at their own observation, speculations, and comments, until it becomes quite apparent that I am getting the worst of it. I retire with a modest unconscious air, which seems to delight them immensely.

Ironed, barricaded, and guarded, as these men are, they sometimes attempt an escape, though without success. Their chief hope often turns upon bribing one of the wardens; for these prisoners—settled for life as they may be—have really the means of bribing. Most of them have gold in Melbourne in care of a friend, or in the banks, or secreted at some of the diggings.

5
Norfolk Island
Irwin and Henry Morley

A detailed description of the Norfolk Island, its occupants and the conduct afforded
each level of the well-defined social order.
Volume: 5 Number: 107 Pages: 73–77
Date: April 10, 1852
Fee: 3 pounds for 7 Columns.

Since residence on Norfolk Island is permitted only to two classes of men;—
namely, to those who are engaged there in the public service, and to those
who, having done the public some disservice, are transported thither in the
character of convicts; and since it is only on occasions of great emergency
that any but a government ship showing the private signals, is permitted to
approach its shore, I take it to be a fact that Norfolk Island does not often
occupy a chapter in books of travel. Now, I have been to Norfolk Island; I
know the place well and the people living there, convicts and all. How I came
by my knowledge is a question which I am not obliged to answer; but, for the
comfort of the clean-fingered, I may state that I am not legally pitch.[1] My
misdeeds have not yet come to be discussed in any court of justice whatever.

   The first glimpse of Norfolk Island that one gets from a ship's deck, is
made remarkable by a tree—well-known by means of pictures and
descriptions—the grand Norfolk Island pine; which clothes the hills to their
summit. The island is of volcanic origin. It is about twenty-one miles in girth,
and rises abruptly from the sea on every side but one. On that one side, of
course, we land. It is a low sandy level—the site of the penal settlement—and

---

[1] Pitch (related to the colour black): villain, felon, black deeds.

not very accessible. The island bids men keep their distance by its physical formation quite as much as by its laws. A coral reef runs round it. Where the coast is inaccessible, the reef lurks under water; but where the coast might otherwise be come at, [approached] the reef shows its teeth and foams at an approaching vessel. It is only at certain times—when the surf beats over the bar in a comparatively placid state of wrath—that any hope of landing can be entertained. The Union Jack hoisted on the flagstaff indicates such a season of relapse, and informs boats that they may attempt to come ashore. The black flag hoisted means: 'If you come now, there is an end of you.'

A boat having arrived, under favourable circumstances, within the reef; having been dashed over the bar very rudely by the wave that crosses it, and tossed down abreast of the jetty; the visitor, when he has fetched his breath, has leisure to observe a gang of convicts, stripped to the waist, with ropes in their hands, ready to plunge in to the rescue, if the boat should happen to capsize. Perhaps the visitor is not allowed to fetch his breath, or to observe this gang, until he has taken a salt-water bath, and has been dragged into society by a rope fastened round his middle. These convicts form the Rescue Gang; and any one of them who saves a life enjoys a shortened period of punishment. If it should happen that the boat is not upset, the visitor stands in it for a little time, tossing on the water near the pier. Then, watching his opportunity, when he is on the top of a wave, he leaps out of the boat into the arms of a Rescue man extended to receive him.

Norfolk Island consists of a series of hills and valleys beautifully interfolded, rising in green ridges one above another, till they all culminate in the summit of Mount Pitt, the highest point in the Island, about three thousand feet above the level of the sea.

The population of the Island is composed of eight hundred convicts, and the local staff essential for their proper management. The free community consists, therefore, wholly of Government officials and their families, together with a military force of about one hundred and fifty men and four or five officers. The good society or first rank of Norfolk Island is composed of the civil commandant, the officers of the garrison, the engineer and commissariat, the two clergymen,—one Protestant, the other Roman Catholic—and a medical officer or two. Superintendents and overseers of convicts make a second rank. Common soldiers are a third rank; and the convicts are, of course, the least respectable.

The capital of Norfolk Island is the gaol. There is, besides, a spacious quadrangle of buildings for the convict barracks, for school-rooms, and for places appointed for divine service. There are commodious barracks for the army of occupation of Norfolk Island. There is the mansion of the commandant, on a beautiful green mound; there are handsome houses for the officials; and, in picturesque, convenient nooks, lurk pleasant cottages for overseers. About three miles from the gaol is Longridge, where a number of prisoners are employed in farming operations. There is also an establishment on the opposite side of the Island called the Cascades, the business of which place is now declining.

From the boundary of the settlement there runs a well-trodden pathway to the Cemetery, which is enclosed on three sides by tear-dropping hedges of the manchineel;[2] and, on the fourth side by a restless mourner, the vexed sea. The climate is healthy, but the graves are numerous and new. A sudden end has closed in this Island many a rugged way of vice. Born in a country which professes to be too religious to give education to its masses, left to be reared in infamy till the day comes—which is so long in coming—when sectarian pride is to give place to Christian charity, the men who sleep here in the graves among the manchineels are to be visited with human sorrow. In me the common graveyard reverence was not the less for want of tombstone eulogies. 'He was a thankless son, a cruel husband, a hard father, and a pot-house[3] friend. Banished for all his burglaries by an indignant country, he lies buried here. His end was violent: he died, in quarrel, by the knife of an associate.' That might be the kind of epitaph which would speak truth among the mounds here, far away in Norfolk Island, about which no foot of wife or sister has been treading.

A large crop of the graves in Norfolk Island has grown out of those attempts at revolt; which formerly were frequent, and could be put down

---

[2] Manchineel: a tropical American tree with poisonous, yellowish-green, apple-like fruit.

[3] Pot-house: alehouse or tavern, especially a disreputable one.

only by brute force. In 1834 a conspiracy was formed; of which the aim was to destroy the military inhabitants by poisoning the wells, and then to put the Island into the possession of the convicts. That was defeated; and thirty-one revolters on that occasion suffered the penalty of death. The last outbreak occurred in 1846. The object on that occasion was to destroy certain overseers who had, by bringing men frequently to punishment, made themselves objects of a wild hate. The leader on this occasion was a certain William Westwood, commonly called Jacky Jacky; that name having been given to him by the natives of New South Wales, when he was leading there a lawless life. By a convict, who was this man's close companion and confederate, I have been favoured with a Newgate calendar[4] of details. Like many of such details, black and repulsive in the mass, they show here and there, through all the mist, a glimmer of that true light of humanity which might have brightened the man's life.

There was indeed some good mixed even with the evil deed that had brought Jacky Jacky into Norfolk Island. Bent upon plunder, he with his associates had visited a settler's house, during the absence of the master. They confined the servants, and proceeded to the best room, in which the lady of the house, with a young lady, her friend, were preparing the children for bed, and perhaps teaching them their prayers. Jacky Jacky stated briefly the object of his visit; and, having left an unaccustomed confederate in charge of the affrighted women, went up-stairs. The report of a gun, followed by screams, called him down again. The lady of the house lay on the floor, surrounded by the children, bleeding profusely from a gunshot wound, which had divided the femoral artery. Jacky Jacky promptly called the whole house to his aid, bound the wound round with sheets as tightly as he could, ordered the settler's horse to be put to the gig; and, as soon as the lady had recovered consciousness, had her placed carefully on cushions at the bottom of the vehicle. Then taking the reins, himself, he quitted his plunder, drove with utmost speed twelve miles to the nearest station; and, knocking up the doctor, committed the wounded lady to his care. Then returning to his followers, he called them off, bidding them not remove an atom from the

---

[4] Newgate calendar: stories of crimes associated with prison.

premises. Upon the information of the man who had fired the gun, according to his own statement, Jacky Jacky and his friends were soon afterwards taken in the Bush. Many crimes having been laid to their charge, they were condemned to death; but by the earnest representations of the lady, who remembered gratefully the considerate distinction he had made in practice between burglary and murder, the sentence was commuted to transportation for life to Norfolk Island. But he was not born to die in his bed. He headed, as I before said, the conspiracy of July, 1846.

Obnoxious constables were to be destroyed and the island to be seized. One morning, immediately after inspection, as the various gangs were being marched to their work, the revolt was opened by a simultaneous rush, and convicts scattered themselves over the settlement in search of their victims;— certain constables who lived in detached cottages near the beach. Those who had been on duty the preceding night, were in one cottage barbarously murdered in their sleep. The soldiery, after much exertion, got the greater number of the convicts back within the gaol; but some were scattered still among the hills, and three or four had seized a boat upon the beach, and made their escape to Philip Island. Philip Island is a lonely rock, lying about six miles from the settlement, inhabited by goats and rabbits, by the seabirds, and by a peculiar kind of green parrot. It is a place occasionally visited by officers of the convict garrison, for a day's shooting. On Philip Island, these three or four men were able for a long time to elude the vigilance of those sent in pursuit; at length, however, all but one were taken, or had thought it prudent to surrender.

For eighteen months that one man, hunted by his fellows, lived on in his desolation, and escaped from every one of the many searching parties sent out to capture him; who were to be heard shouting about the rock from time to time—the only human voices that disturbed his solitude. At length his lair was discovered. The desperate man then climbed swiftly to the highest pinnacle of rock in the small island. There he quietly awaited his pursuers. With much toil they had nearly scaled the height on which he stood: he gave them a wild look of hatred and defiance, covered his head with his jacket, and leapt down, rebounding from rock to rock, and falling a shattered mass into the sea. What was his mother doing then in England?

For this outbreak, seventy convicts were put on their trial; and of the seventy, thirteen, including Jacky Jacky, were condemned to death. They lie together in one grave, upon unconsecrated ground outside the cemetery, close to the rocky shore where the waves beat upon the coral reef. They had been tried by a commission sent from Sydney. Until then, all persons charged with capital offences had been shipped to Sydney for trial; but that practice was dropped, in order that there might no longer exist a motive which had been a strange and frequent source of crime. The old hardened convicts had amused themselves by urging the new-comers into conflict with each other; and inciting them to murder their companions, in order that they—the instigators—might have evidence to give, and thus get the relief of a voyage to Sydney in the character of witnesses.

My talk has wandered from the cemetery; but I must come back to it and read one tombstone, sacred to the memory of Thomas Salisbury Wright, who was transported from Sydney at the age of one hundred and three for the term of his natural life. So here he died, having completed his one hundred and fifth year. To be sure he was a young man when he committed the forgery for which he was transported. That occurred when he was only eighty-three years old.

Through a cutting in the ledge of rock which overhangs the sea, I come now upon an amphitheatre of hills. These hills are all richly dressed in a thick clothing of wild shrubs, flowers, and grapery. On one side is a mount covered to the top with the gigantic Norfolk Island pine; on another side down goes a ravine that seems to offer a short cut to the interior of the earth: a short and a most pleasant cut; for intricate dark foliage is lighted up by lemon groves, where, here and there, the sun is playing on their golden fruit. I descend by the path into the ravine. Foliage shuts me out from the sun; magnificent creepers (for in nature, as in society, there are creepers which take rank as the magnificent) twist and twirl themselves about my path. The birds that perch upon them glitter like their flowers: lories, parrots, parroquets, beautiful wood-pigeons. But the forest is dark, and I ascend again, and get among such quaint aspects of vegetative life as are made by clusters of large fern trees, rising with a lean—some to this quarter and some to that—trees sadly wanting in uprightness of character, but carrying their crests fifteen or twenty feet above the ground. These look like grass among the Norfolk Island pines, which pile one dark feather-crown upon another—crown above crown, to a height of some two hundred feet above the soil.

From the summit of Mount Pitt, which I have now reached, I have Norfolk Island in complete subjection to one of my senses. I can see it all. Rock, forest, valley, cornfields, islets, sunshine on sea, sunshine on birds, no sun in gloomy glades, rays darting into darkness, and revealing parasites and creepers exquisitely coloured, and the bright green fans of the palmetto[5] rising out of a froth of white convolvulus;[6] guava and lemon, a delicious air, clear sky, and the sharp outline of every light feather of the foliage picked out against it.

There used to be oranges; but, once upon a time, there lived in Norfolk Island a wise commandant, who voted oranges too great a luxury for convicts, and caused the trees that grew them to be extirpated. They are now, however, being reintroduced. In a garden belonging to the commandant, called Orange Vale, sight, taste, and smell enjoy a paradise. Delicate cinnamon grows by the rough stout old English oak. Tea, coffee, tobacco, sugarcane, banana, figs, arrowroot and lemon grow in company with English fruits and vegetables that have been forced by the climate into an ecstatic, transcendental state. The spirituality of a carrot gets to be developed when it grows up in such good company as that of sweet bucks and bananas. Sweet bucks are sweet potatoes, which are very kisses to the palate; and are served out daily as rations to the evil and the good, the convicts and the officers.

But truly there is need of a fine climate to make compensation for the other details of a residence in Norfolk Island—I do not mean to the convicts who are cut off here from all the rest of mankind, and whose case is deplorable; but to those who guard and govern them. The members of the local staff form but a limited field of social intercourse for one another. The 'Lady Franklin' is the only regular trader to their little coast from Hobart Town (one thousand three hundred miles away); she makes but four trips in

---

[5] Palmetto: several species of palm growing in the West Indies and southern United States.
[6] Convolvulus: a trailing plant with funnel-shaped flowers.

the year. A convict ship is not often sent on from England. When a ship does arrive on lawful business at Norfolk Island, great is the sensation. The coming in of a ship on business causes, apparently, all business to be at an end. Letters from home bless the temporary exiles; for they have to be enjoyed and answered. All in the ship who are entertainable are hospitably to be entertained. In private and in public life, who is alive and who is dead in England; who is up and who is down; what bubbles have burst, and what new bubbles have been blown, have to be learned over the dinner-table. The highest virtue of a visitor is untiring loquacity.

The dark scenes of convict life, of which I have already given some examples, do not now fill Norfolk Island with their ancient honours. Here also the good old times have given way to better new times. Captain Macconochie, under all the difficulties against which he had to contend when he was governor, utterly broke down the old ferocious system. Under the temperate, strict, and judicious control of Mr. Price, the present commandant, a system of discipline has been established; which, while it does not make the probation of the convicts other than a term of punishment, accords to them such wholesome management, and such fair treatment, as has humanised their conduct among one another, and towards those set in authority over them. Formerly, in the blaze of noonday, it was dangerous for any one to walk alone beyond the precincts of the settlement. Violent crimes and murders were common among the gangs while at their work—convict quarrelling with convict. The resident was clouded with a daily sense of insecurity, a dread for the safety of his wife or children when they left his sight.˜

For then the incessant lash made hard hearts harder; and wretches made to grovel in dark cells, chained by ring-bolts to the floor, and wearing sixty pounds of iron on their arms, were degraded even lower than they had been forced at home below the feelings of humanity. Then convicts were driven at night-fall, besmeared and dirty with the day's toil, into the barrack, and were locked up till morning in neglected rooms, to prey upon each other. No officer who ventured there among them would come out alive; but, in front of the open grated windows sentries paced, whose orders were to fire promptly into any room from which the sound of tumult or the cry of murder should proceed, if the disturbance did not cease at his command. Whether the shot went into the body of the right offender, was a lottery which rendered it the interest of all, if possible—but among men so brutalised, how was it possible?—to check the violent.

Now, this is all changed for the better. Still the discipline is very strict; and so works, which it is to the most hardened the most severe in punishment. The sleeping-rooms are now well lighted and well ventilated. The two hours between supper and rest have been spent in the school, and the day has been closed with prayers. The two clergymen, Messrs. Batchelor and Ryan—one Protestant, one Roman Catholic—each in his sphere work without intermission. The schools are well-conducted; and, where they awaken, as they do in most, a desire for knowledge, they beget a mutual confidence between the well-conducted, who now form by far the chief proportion of the convicts. Locks and bolts are falling out of use upon the doors of the residents; and, because there are few female servants, pretty children—children thrive and look unusually pretty in a climate such as this—may be seen carried on the arms of house-breakers, or drawn in their small carts through the lemon groves and gardens, by the brown, rugged hands that had grown hard in deeds of violence.

It is no miracle that has been here performed; men bred to crime in England by the ignorance and filth we cherish, are bred out of crime again in Norfolk Island, by a little teaching and a little human care. Almost all the men who return to Hobart Town after fulfilling their term of probation here, are in demand as servants, and are preferred to fresh arrivers from the mother-country. Stepmother-country she is to an immense proportion of her children!

6
Transported for Life [Part One]
William Moy Thomas

An account of William Henry Barber, a solicitor (whose name is not revealed in the article), who was transported to Norfolk Island in 1844. The article describes his imprisonment, trial and subsequent conviction, followed by his transfer by ship to Norfolk Island. See notes at the end of part two for more details on Barber.
Volume: 5 Number: 123 Pages: 455–64
Date: July 31, 1852
Fee: 10 pounds 10 shillings for 18 Columns.

The following narrative is not fictitious. It has been taken down from the lips of the narrator, whose sufferings are described; with the object of showing what Transportation, at the present time, really is.

Many years ago—eventful years with me—I stood at the bar of a court of justice, and heard the terrible announcement of the judge, that I was to be transported to a penal colony for the remainder of my life. My innocence of the crime of which twelve men had, at the end of my long trial, declared me guilty, has since been established. I have not forgotten, nor shall I ever forget, with what emotions I rose, at the end of a trial which lasted a whole week, to make my last appeal, 'in arrest of judgment.' My appeal was in vain; and, when I heard my principal fellow prisoner whom I then knew to be guilty, asserting in fewer words—though with scarcely less fervour—that he also was guiltless, I felt how little the most emphatic assertions of a prisoner could weigh with those who have had long experience in the administration of justice. Then, and not till then, a feeling of my utter helplessness came upon me. The complete isolation of the soul of every man from me had never before presented itself so strongly to my mind. My fellow prisoner has since acquitted me of all participation in his crime. How different, then, were the thoughts and feelings in our breasts, as we stood there side by side. Yet the crowd about us were as unable to look into the mind of the guilty man, as I was powerless to make known to them my own.~

The present separate celled prison omnibus had not come into use at that time; and, after the trial was over, myself and a batch of other prisoners were conveyed from Newgate in a long van open at the top and guarded by a policeman, in the place of conductor, to the prison at Milbank. I was chained leg to leg with a man who had been twice convicted of burglary. The operation of riveting on the irons is a painful one, and is performed with as much rudeness and with as little feeling as it could have been done five centuries since—each stroke of the riveting hammer causing a sensation of pain something like toothdrawing. It was a fine spring morning; and through the entrance of the vehicle, I caught a glimpse—perhaps, as I thought, for the last time—of the busy streets, already growing strange to me after the three months' imprisonment which preceded my trial. I thought of how often I had passed through those very streets, as free and happy as any of the throng I saw there. Some stood to look at our vehicle; though most were too busy to take any heed of us. The sun was shining; the shopkeepers, here and there, were unfurling their street blinds, or watering the pavement in front of their doors. A water-cart had passed over one part of our route, and the air seemed so fresh to me, who had been used to the close atmosphere of a prison cell, that I could have shut my eyes and fancied myself in the country. The narrow strip of sky between the two lines of houses which we were able to observe above our roofless vehicle seemed bluer than it had ever been before: the colours of the shops were brighter; the people in the streets, men, women, and children, more neat and clean than when I had seen them last. A business-like air was in the countenances of most of them. Every one seemed to be charged with an errand. I almost wondered to see them wending so gravely towards the city on such a fine morning. Yet how often I had been one of them; and had never dreamed, unless by predetermination, of wandering away into the country on such a fine day to enjoy that liberty, of which I had never truly known the value until then.

It was indeed many a day before I saw again anything so refreshing as the sight of the streets in that half-hour's ride. At Milbank I remained about two months. Meanwhile I heard nothing of what had passed in the world outside the walls of my prison—what was the public opinion upon my sentence; or whether the efforts of my few friends on my behalf were likely to prove successful. One night, however, I learnt from a turnkey[1]—a kind-hearted man—that one of my fellow prisoners (not the principal one) had confessed his guilt, and had exonerated me from all participation in it: but I heard no more. Nothing occurred to show that this circumstance exercised a favourable influence over my fate. Indeed, I knew that such confessions have ordinarily little effect. I was, therefore, not surprised when I heard from the officer on duty, as he looked into my cell one night, that we were to be removed early on the following morning.

At about four o'clock we were accordingly called forth, and ordered to put on an entirely new suit of clothes, consisting of a coarse brown serge[2] jacket, waistcoat, breeches, stockings, highlows,[3] and a particularly frightful skull-cap. All the articles appeared to have been selected at random, without the slightest reference to the dimensions of the wearer; the jacket would have enveloped two such bodies as mine, and the breeches scarcely came down to my knees. A few minutes were allowed for the slipping on of these garments; after which every man received a hunch of bread, and we were equipped for a voyage of seventeen thousand miles. We were formed in line, and handcuffed two and two; a heavy iron chain, in addition, being passed through a ring of the handcuff, so as to fasten about a dozen of us together. The signal was then given to march; and we proceeded, under a strong guard of the prison officers with muskets loaded, down to the river side in front of the prison, to embark.

Notwithstanding the early hour, a number of persons were there to watch the process of embarkation. Whatever may be said of the failure of the Government in the systems for the treatment of convicts, they have been

---

[1] Turnkey: a gaoler, one who has charge of keys and a prison.
[2] Serge: woolen fabric.
[3] Highlows: a laced ankle-high boot.

eminently successful in rendering their appearance abject and pitiable: when to the ugliness of the clothing was added the total disregard of bulk and stature, the appearance of some of our party was perfectly ludicrous. The nether garments of one man, intended to reach to the knee, only had to be buttoned a little above his ankles; whilst those of others did not extend to the knee. Two hundred and twenty of us were conveyed in three drafts on board a steamer in waiting to convey us. Our boat contained seventy. I could not help thinking of water parties of a different character; but, upon the whole, my mind was more tranquil than I could have expected. I endeavoured, as far as possible, to step out of myself and to speculate upon the history and character of those who, with one exception, were strangers to me; but who were now to be my companions by night and day, for at least four months; and to wonder if there was one among them with whom I might hope to beguile the long and wearisome days and nights of the coming voyage.

At Milbank we had been kept upon the silent and solitary system. The restraint being removed aboard the steamer, every man seemed determined to make up for lost time. Many had been former acquaintances, and had a world of news to exchange. Nothing could have produced a stranger effect than their conduct, contrasted with their abject appearance, condition, and prospects. They laughed, jested, and sang; and, despite the chains with which they were loaded, some of them even danced. My nearest neighbour was one of the merriest. He exulted in the many escapes he had had, and in the fact that, after all, he was only transported for ten years.

At Woolwich we were put aboard the convict ship; every man as he descended into the hold being numbered on the back, like one of a flock of sheep. The centre of the vessel was appropriated to the prisoners, and was divided into compartments, each accommodating eight men, with a square table and seats of portable deal[4] boards, arranged in tiers—above and below—all round. At night these were so disposed as to form sleeping berths. If any one will imagine a long room filled with pauper coffins with the lids off, he will have a good idea of our dormitory. Our irons were immediately knocked off; but, on the following morning, we were one at a time

---

[4] Deal: fir or pine timber boards.

summoned on deck and ironed more heavily, having a ring round the ankle, with a long heavy chain attached to another ring. This we dragged about with us till my leg was severely excoriated; and getting in and out of my sleeping berth, and going up and down the ladder became a difficult task. I have since learnt that it is not usual to chain prisoners on the voyage, except for misconduct; and I believe that my fellow-prisoners had to attribute this to the accident of my being among their number. But if they thus suffered on my account, Heaven knows I suffered enough on theirs during the voyage; for petty offences were frequently committed, of which the particular authors could not be detected; consequently, all were punished by increased privations.‾

During our stay at Woolwich, the prisoners were allowed to write to their friends, and to take a last farewell of those who might choose to visit them, although strangers were compelled to remain in a boat alongside, and were not allowed to come aboard. So disfigured were they by their dress and close cut hair, that wives could scarcely recognise their own husbands. A gentleman who had known me from childhood said, 'If I had not heard your voice, I could not believe it was yourself.' Excepting some affecting leave-takings, the time here was spent in great hilarity. Some of the prisoners' friends brought them a little money; and it was mysteriously hinted to me by one of the officers of the vessel, that a round Dutch cheese, scooped out and filled with sovereigns, would be found useful; but I was unable to avail myself of his counsel. Some tea, which was afterwards stolen from me, and a few shillings were all my viaticum.[5] There was a subscription for a violin; but it was subsequently found that no one was capable of playing on it. Nevertheless, without music and with a heavy chain clanking to one leg, some danced as merrily as if they had been in a booth at a fair. They were also allowed to make purchases of the 'bumboat-man,'[6] who appeared to enjoy a monopoly of this branch of Government patronage. He supplied a variety of trifling articles, such as cakes, fruit, needles, thread, tin plates, &c.,

---

[5] Viaticum: provisions, money or supplies for a journey.
[6] Bumboat: a boat that brings provisions and commodities for sale to a larger ship in port or offshore.

at a profit of about one hundred and fifty per cent.; but his customers contrived to square the account in a way peculiarly their own; for, while he was extorting an undue profit on the one hand, his basket was generally robbed by adroit thieves on the other.

In the river, our rations consisted of biscuits, soup, and cocoa, night and morning. At sea, we had salt meat with a pudding—pleasantly termed plum-pudding—but he was lucky indeed who found a plum in his slice. On alternate days we had pork and pea-soup. Each man received an iron spoon and a tin pot, but no plates, knives or forks. Upon a kind hint from the surgeon (who is the representative of Government in a convict ship), I had purchased a tin plate, although, as I was the only member of my mess who indulged in this luxury, it exposed me to some coarse ridicule; but as I bore this with good humour, my companions (seven more desperate characters could not well have been found) were soon reconciled to me and my tin plate. The food was delivered to one of every eight men, who were called the captain of the mess. He then divided it—meat or pudding—into eight lots; and these were laid in two rows on the mess table. To prevent partiality, one [member] of the mess was selected to name the several owners, turning his back, whilst another, placing his hand on the tempting lump, cried out 'Who shall?' I subsequently, however, discovered that under this ostentatious parade of fair play there lurked the grossest injustice; for having noticed that both the parties engaged in dealing out 'even handed justice,' always got the largest portions, and that their office was regarded as a privilege, I was led to inquire of one of the mess during the voyage, and learnt that there was a well understood confederacy between the adjudicators.

Our ship was of five hundred and sixty tons burden; and besides the ordinary complement of seamen, carried a military guard of fifty men. The entire management of the two hundred and twenty prisoners was confided to the surgeon, whose duties were both arduous and dangerous; for it was impossible for him to avoid incurring the ill-will of some of the more desperate characters. We had also a chaplain, who read prayers every day in the prison when the sea was not too rough; and on Sundays performed divine service on deck, which we all attended.

The day fixed for our departure had (as is customary) been studiously concealed from us. One morning we were towed down the river, and about two miles out into the Channel. The time passed at Woolwich—from the corresponding with friends, dealings with the bumboat-man, the temporary enjoyment of little luxuries of which they had been long deprived; the revival of old acquaintances, the exchange of news and of messages, the eager examination of newspapers occasionally, though secretly, introduced—was one of comparative enjoyment to most of the prisoners. But there were those who, like myself, clung to the hope that they would yet be snatched from the abyss of misery which lay before them. The bumboat-man's basket had no attraction for them, nor could they enjoy any of the gratifications placed for a moment within their reach. They corresponded continually with their friends, scanned with eager anxiety every boat that came alongside, and observed with wistful eye every post delivery. Circumstances did justify hopes in some; but they sank as the vessel got rapidly out to sea. Still many clung to them; adverse winds might keep us in the Downs, where a countermand might yet be received. These hopes were, however, in no case realised. Order and quiet was now maintained; but the men generally were much depressed as we gradually lost sight of land, and began to speculate upon the sufferings which awaited them. Our place of destination was generally understood (although that was kept as secret as possible) to be Norfolk Island.

Once at sea, and every hope being cut off for the present, I resolved to submit myself as cheerfully as possible to my strange fate, and to endeavour to be useful to my fellow prisoners; trusting that my life might be spared through the dangers of a long sea voyage, and the hardships of a penal settlement, until that day of justice and reinstatement in society which I never doubted would, sooner or later, arrive. I was made librarian, chaplain's clerk, and inspector of the night watch; so that, although my miseries were neither few nor trifling, the want of occupation was not one of the number. The books constituting the library were supplied by various charitable societies; they were selected with care, being confined to religious and scientific subjects popularly treated, excluding such as would convey information that was likely to be misapplied. Many were on natural history with plates, and these were much sought after by those who could not read—a large proportion. Our books were a blessing, and I am persuaded had a good effect upon the minds and feelings. There were about one hundred volumes, great and small; and, notwithstanding they were in constant circulation, there was not one deficient at the end of the voyage.

The authorities aboard were very jealous of books upon nautical and geographical subjects. On one occasion the captain, noticing a volume of 'Guthrie's Geography' in a prisoner's hand, immediately seized and threw it overboard. It was supposed that information might be derived from such sources which would tempt the prisoners to endeavour to take the ship, and effect their escape; and, in truth, the practicability of this was a favourite topic; especially with those who had been transported before, and who had pretty accurate information as to instances of both success and failure in the seizing of ships, as well by crews as by convicts. Our irons had been taken off on first getting to sea, and it was said that the capture of the ship, and an escape to the coast would be easy, if the prisoners were true to each other. The successful seizure of the Wellington by convicts on its way from Sydney to Norfolk Island, as well as the famous mutiny of the Bounty, were quoted as instances of the facility with which the object might be accomplished. It was generally believed that a sudden rush upon the poop[7] would settle the matter—that the sentinels would, in a moment, be overpowered and disarmed. Amongst the prisoners were several old sailors who, it was believed, would be able to steer the ship should the mates prove refractory. Nothing, I believe, prevented the attempt but the consciousness that there were those among themselves who would have been as much opposed to their design as the captain himself, and who would have frustrated it, if there had been any serious intention of carrying it into execution. Before we were well out of the Channel we encountered a severe gale, which carried away

---

[7] Poop: a raised deck at the stern of a sailing ship that sometimes forms the roof of a cabin: also, poop deck.

our foretop-gallant mast[8] and royal.[9] A great number of the prisoners were sea-sick. When it is remembered how wretched is the saloon of even a first-class steamer occupied by the most civilised of human beings, with convenient berths, attentive stewards, and all suitable appliances, some faint, but very inadequate idea, may be gained of the loath-some and miserable circumstances in which I was placed, with one-third of our party sea-sick, and no provision made for such a state of things.

We had not been a month at sea when the small-pox broke out amongst us; although, by the exertions of the medical officer, it was confined to six of our number. A young man, whom I had previously remarked as one of the finest and most robust-looking aboard, fell a victim. He was committed to the deep in the usual manner; the church service being read by the chaplain, and I acting as clerk. All the prisoners were assembled on deck, and many of them seemed affected. For myself I rejoiced that, although a transported convict, and in spite of my degrading dress and miserable condition, I could respond without shame to the beautiful prayers of the burial service. The rest recovered; and, after this, the general health was very good. We had no vegetables, except some preserved potatoes, which only lasted three weeks.

Before we arrived at the Cape we kept too far out at sea to catch more than shadowy glimpses of the land; these, however, sufficed for topics of conversation, especially as we were enabled to learn from day to day the exact progress we made. The most distinct view we obtained of any land was of Gough's Island, in 40 degrees, 19 minutes latitude, and 7 degrees, 30 minutes west longitude; six days after sighting which we bore up for the Cape, at the request of the surgeon, who represented to the captain that the health of the prisoners required rest and the support of fresh provisions for a few days. Flights of pigeons indicated the approach of land, though still five hundred miles distant. The water lost its deep blue tint, and the swell of the

---

[8] Foretop: a platform at the head of a ship's foremast (the mast nearest to the bow; the front or curved end of a vessel); foretop-gallant mast: the mast above the foremast, and at the head of which stands the foretop-gallant mast.
[9] Royal mast: a small mast next to the top-gallant mast; royal: a small sail set on the royal mast used only in light breezes.

waves grew less and less. We entered Symon's Bay seventy-one days after leaving Woolwich. When one lynx-eyed man declared he could see a team of four horses with a driver, his assertion produced a loud laugh; but when its motion was distinctly observable, and nearer approach confirmed the fact that it actually was a man driving a waggon with four horses, the excitement was immense. The weather was very fine. The bay is in the form of a horse-shoe, shut in with mountains, the slopes of which are green to the water's edge, and dotted far and wide with white villas.

Figure 1.4 Chain gang: convicts going to work near Sydney NSW by Edward Backhouse, c.1842. Image courtesy of Allport Library and Museum of Fine Arts, Tasmanian Archive and Heritage Office: AUTAS001124070970.

I cannot express the intense desire I felt to land and to explore the regions beyond those mountains; which, to my imagination, concealed a paradise. I would at that moment have accepted my liberty, even if the country had been inhabited by cannibals. I cannot, therefore, be surprised—with the beautiful shores stretched so temptingly around us—at the numerous plans of escape which were anxiously discussed during the few days we remained in the bay;

especially as it was the first and last time in the course of the voyage that such a temptation would occur. A party of four of the prisoners made a desperate effort. Three of them were employed about the ship, and had, therefore, facilities for making arrangements for flight. They were not compelled to descend into the prison dungeon, like the rest of us, an hour before sunset. The fourth answered to his name at the evening muster, but slipped back instead of descending the ladder, and concealed himself upon deck until midnight; when all four glided stealthily down the ship's side, and struck out for the shore. Whether they eluded the sentinels, or were in collusion with them, was not known; but, as it was one of the brilliant moonlight nights of those latitudes, and the bay was perfectly calm, they could hardly have escaped the observation of the sentinels on duty.˜

The vessel lay at anchor in the centre of the bay, which at that part is three miles broad; so that land, at the nearest point, which they could hardly have ventured to approach—guard being constantly on duty there—was a mile and a half distant. But they calculated upon getting rest upon the anchor chains of other vessels lying between our ship and the shore. They found their strength, however, less than they had expected, for they had not allowed for the weakening effects of a two months' voyage upon wretched and unvaried diet. Three of them turned back, and with great difficulty regained the ship—indeed, but for the help of one of them, who was a good swimmer and a man of extraordinary muscular power, the other two would have been drowned. The fourth man firmly refused to turn back, preferring, as he said, death itself to Norfolk Island. The three who returned were found at daylight upon deck, their clothes saturated with the salt water, and were reported. The surgeon, upon discovering the escape of one of his men was much excited; information was given to the authorities ashore; scouts were despatched to Cape Town, and in all directions, but no tidings were obtained of the runaway. By some it was conjectured that he had been snapped under by one of the sharks with which the bay abounds. This was the man to whom I had been chained leg to leg at Newgate. He had been a steward on board a ship, and had frequently been at Cape Town. There is no doubt, therefore, that he had planned all along to get away at this point. He was transported a second time for housebreaking; the commission of which crime he did not deny.

Indeed, it was by no means usual for the prisoners among themselves to deny their guilt; nor was there any inducement to do so. On the contrary, such a pretence, if credited, only produced distrust, from the want of community of feeling, views, interests, and principles, which form the only bond among those unhappy men. A convict who said, 'I am innocent,' was in danger of the fate of the white crow, whose brethren picked out his eyes simply from the different colour of his plumage.

Like all the other offences of my fellow-captives, this escape drew down upon the whole of us increased privations. The surgeon hastened our departure; and, during the rest of our stay, we were almost always kept below; getting only an occasional peep at the magnificent coast through the port-holes. We were restricted from making little purchases—which had been permitted before—of oranges, eggs, salt fish, and Cape wine; all of which were extremely cheap, and were brought alongside by a very fine specimen of the Hottentot race, who spoke English about as well as the Chinese Comprador at Canton, or the market women at Boulogne or Calais. Nearly all my leisure, during my stay here, was spent in writing letters to my friends and to persons of influence in England; no less than nineteen of which I despatched by different opportunities.

On the seventh day after entering this beautiful bay a favourable breeze sprang up, and we set sail for Norfolk Island. After doubling the Cape, we got into the Trade Winds; which continued with us—although at times very light almost to a dead calm—for the rest of our voyage. Flights of albatrosses and other sea birds accompanied us; wheeling about the ship in graceful circles, and occasionally darting down and soaring up again with some small fish in their beaks. To shoot them was a favourite amusement with the civil and military officers aboard.

We had left the Cape about three weeks, when there was a general murmuring among the men, which some of the more desperate sought to kindle into open mutiny. At the commencement of our voyage, there had been exhibited on deck a table showing the rations to which we were entitled under the contractor's agreement with the Government; and in it was the item of 'two gallons of wine each,' to be given in the course of the voyage. This had a smack of luxury with it which seemed out of keeping with the rest of our miserable dietary; but experience had shown that prisoners became so reduced by a four months' voyage, crowded together to suffocation, as absolutely to require some slight stimulant, and accordingly this modicum of wine (Cape) was ordered, and came under the head of 'Medical comforts.' This had been served out to each man mixed with lime juice—a gill[10] at a time, once a week. As even the allowance had not commenced until we had been some time at sea, it was evident that, at this rate, there would be a large surplus at the end of the voyage. We were in about 40 degrees of latitude; and, with our slender clothing and reduced condition, suffered severely from cold. The more evil-disposed insisted that keeping back the wine was a deliberate fraud—a foretaste of the cruelty and injustice in store for them, and hinted that any fate was better than Norfolk Island, where all chance of escape would be cut off. They compared their own strength with the military guard, counted up many soldiers and sailors who would, they believed, desert to their side upon the first outbreak. I observed more attention was paid to these dangerous suggestions than formerly; and, amongst a considerable party of the oldest prisoners, there seemed a more fixed and serious purpose.˜

Thinking it probable that the surgeon, who had shown great zeal and humanity hitherto, had proper reasons for reserving the wine, I was loath to interfere; but the aspect of affairs was every day becoming more alarming. Men left their berths and debated in clusters, for hours together, various schemes for seizing the ship. In this state of things, I suggested that we should respectfully memorialise the surgeon on the subject. My proposal was at first very jeeringly received; but some of the better disposed approving of it, the rest agreed, believing, and I fear hoping, that the memorial would be treated as an impertinence, and thus fan the flame they had kindled. I immediately prepared an address; expressing our gratitude for the medical skill and kindness we had received, and respectfully stating our complaint as to the wine. This being signed by the captain of each of the different messes on behalf of the whole, I forwarded it to the surgeon, with a note stating the circumstances which had induced me to interfere. In a few minutes he came

---

[10] Gill: a measure for liquids, containing a quarter of a standard pint.

down, and said that withholding the wine was the result of a miscalculation, and assured us that we should receive the remainder in double allowances daily for the future—a promise which he faithfully observed. This kept the men in good humour for the rest of the voyage; and the evil counsels that were every now and then repeated by some of the most desperate, failed of their intended effect.

Between the Cape and Norfolk Island, a distance of about ten thousand miles, we only sighted one sail, which was believed to be an American whaler. I had hoped to catch a glimpse of the little volcanic island of St. Pauls; but, for the sake of a stronger and steadier wind, our Captain kept [to] a much higher latitude than is usual, and we passed the island at about three hundred miles to the south.

Among my two hundred and twenty companions, I found one—I am sorry to say only one—in whose society and conversation I found solace and amusement. He was a fine young man, with an intelligent countenance, and not quite twenty-one years of age. His was a sad story. He had been a merchant's clerk, and in an evil hour had been tempted by the offer of a promising speculation to create himself a capital by forging acceptances. These he renewed as they became due, until an accident led to his detection. He had a young wife, to whom he had been married only three months. On the very night of his apprehension he had been reading aloud to her 'The Diary of a late Physician;' and, having finished one of the short stories he turned the page, and his eye caught the title of the next. It was the episode of the 'Forger.' He hesitated a moment; but, as he told me, he felt his wife's eye upon him, and a guilty fear of awakening her suspicions compelled him to read on. The details of the story sank deep into his heart, and he observed with a superstitious dread his wife's intense interest in the hero of the narrative. He had not laid down the book an hour, when the officers of justice arrived: he was torn from his wife, tried, and convicted.—He had read extensively, and possessed an extraordinary memory—would to Heaven that all who are tempted to sin, as he had sinned, might picture to themselves his mental suffering! Sometimes we spent many hours of the night together, standing at the foot of our berths, discoursing of every conceivable subject that could serve to lift him for awhile above the feeling of his degraded position; but there were periods when he sank into a low despondency for days together. In vain I sought to cheer him with the prospect of future liberty, and an honourable career that should atone for past error; far away from the scene of his first crime.

We had now left England three months; yet this period seemed to me a life of misery, to which all my previous career was but a short prologue. My sufferings, both mental and physical, had much weakened me, and there were times when I found it hard to keep that hopeful and patient tone of mind, with which I had tried to go through the voyage. It was monstrous and incredible (I thought) that I, who had never offended against the laws of my country, should be there suffering the most terrible punishment, short of death, which had been devised for the worst of ruffians; and when my mind was overwrought by this thought I marvelled at the tameness with which I had endured it. I remember once endeavouring to trace those ideas of the duty of bearing injustice with patience, to their origin; and, it seemed to me, that I had been cheating myself all along with the maxims of those who had never suffered as I had, or had even imagined such a case as mine. These gloomy thoughts visited me mostly at night-time; and, although the morning generally brought with it a calmer feeling and a more reasonable consideration of the uselessness of anything I might say or do to ameliorate my condition, I could not help, while the mood lasted, feeling impatient and discontented with myself, as if I had 'lacked gall to make oppression bitter.'

My dreams since my conviction had been almost invariably of a painful nature. The bustle of the day, and the routine of duties to which I had now become accustomed, served to occupy my mind; but, on finding myself alone, the feeling of my misfortunes weighed heavily upon me, and in my sleep this sense seemed to give birth to every possible variety of fearful and distressing imagination. Once, and once only, do I distinctly remember dreaming of my former condition. It was on the night after we had been promised the increased allowance of wine. This trifling piece of good fortune, and the satisfaction I felt in having removed a cause of discontent breaking the dreary monotony of convict life, was sufficient to beget in me better spirits. My hopes for the future grew brighter that night, and the miseries of the past seemed to me soon about to be forgotten in happier times. Thus, in spite of the intense cold, and our scanty bed clothing, I fell asleep. Then it was, that with no fear of the gun of the sentry, or the hard life-struggle with the waves which had probably overcome my unhappy comrade, I slipped away from that dungeon floating on the wide ocean; and, in an instant, retracing all our long and wearisome voyage, was again in England, in my old home.˜

There was little remarkable in the dream itself. I was merely living again one of the ordinary days of my previous life. But how strange that there was no presentiment of coming evil, no wonderment at my own intense delight in the commonest things of life! How strange to have been shown the time to come, with all its terrible experiences; and then to drink a Lethe draught,[11] and slipping back again, to have no memory of it—every thought and recollection of what I had suffered shuffled off with my degrading garments, and left behind in that gloomy ship's hold; where, but a moment before, I had lain down to sleep with my miserable companions. I was at home. Faces of old friends were there. The same furniture was about the room, the same pictures upon the walls; but the table was strewn with strange books in rich and curious binding, which I was examining and wondering how they came there. Blessed dream! not a whit less sweet or real while it lasted than if its magic flight and freedom had been true.

I do not know how long this fancy lasted, but I think I had been dreaming all the time I had been asleep. At all events I was still amid the same scene, when I felt some one shake me, and heard a voice calling me by name. No wonder that the spell was broken at the well-known sound of that voice. It was the man whom I loathed as the author of all my misfortunes, and with whom I had been supposed to have been associated in guilt. I had not known that it was his turn to watch that night, for I had studiously avoided all intercourse with him from the day of my sentence. It was the duty of the watchman to awaken me to relieve him, and thus, by a strange fatality,

---

[11] Lethe draught: in Greek and Roman mythology; one who drank from the river of Hades would become forgetful and not remember their former life; oblivion, forgetfulness.

it fell to him to arouse me from the only dream of happiness vouchsafed to me during the voyage.

It may be of interest to the reader to know something of the routine of management of the convicts on the voyage. The medical superintendent, as I have mentioned, is invested with absolute control over the prisoners, and is responsible for their safety. He was assisted in our vessel by two overseers who had been non-commissioned officers in the army, and were to be overseers in Norfolk Island: one of them was, by his own account, as profligate and unprincipled a vagabond as ever I met with. The most recent piece of scoundrelism which this officer—selected for carrying out the great probation system—frequently related and chuckled over to the prisoners, was a promise of marriage he had made to a servant, who was to accompany him to enjoy his 'colonial appointment,' and by which he had got her watch and several years' savings. The latter fact was considered highly amusing, and contributed not a little to his popularity. He had promised to marry her on a day when he knew that the ship would have been at least a week at sea. As it eventually turned out, the maiden was not so easily disposed of; for she took a passage shortly after in another ship; and, on her arrival in the colony demanded the fulfilment of his promise, under pain of an exposure; which it seems the wretch had not the courage to brave. Whether matrimony, under the circumstances, made either of the parties happy, is more than I can say.

At six o'clock every morning, the prison door was unlocked by one of these overseers, who called out 'Beds up!' whereupon every man arose from his berth, rolled up his bedding—consisting of a thin mattress and one blanket, and took them on deck, where they remained all day to be aired. Then the floor of the prison was scraped and swept in turns by the prisoners who did not fulfil any special office—such as schoolmaster, clerk, captain of the mess. The captains received the day's rations for their respective messes. Those who liked it got something of a wash with salt water, introduced from the forecastle[12] with a leathern pipe. Ablutions performed under such difficulties led to many practical jokes, and not a few battles. At eight o'clock, a pint of cocoa was served out to each man; which, with his biscuit, made his

---

[12] Forecastle: the upper deck of a ship in front of the foremast.

breakfast. Immediately afterwards school was commenced, books were distributed, and exchanged; the surgeon examined the sick, heard complaints, and awarded punishments. These consisted of confinement below deck, heavy chains, or, imprisonment in a kind of sentry box on deck, resembling a Chinese cage, in which the inmate can neither sit, lie down, nor stand upright. We had only one case of flogging. In the afternoon, we usually had prayers read by the chaplain; sometimes with a moral exordium, which was delivered in an impressive and earnest manner.˜

At five o'clock we had a pint of tea. Neither our tea nor our cocoa bore much resemblance to the beverages which I had previously known under those names; but they were warm and comforting. At six o'clock the beds were taken down and arranged; and at half-past six we were mustered, and returned, one by one to our prison, where we were locked in—a sentinel, with loaded musket and fixed bayonet, being placed at the door. Our night was thus nearly twelve hours long. It being too dark to read, and as it was impossible to sleep much more than half the time, I was compelled, for four or five hours every night, to hear little else than narratives of offences and criminal indulgences, of the most revolting character. Obscene and blasphemous songs were nightly composed and sung; and schemes for future crimes were proposed and discussed, with a coolness which I shudder to call to mind. The only check on them was the sentinel at the door, who now and then thrust his bayonet between the bars, when it was getting very late or the men were unusually uproarious, and called out 'silence.'

Our voyage occupied one hundred and twenty-four days; and—when it is considered that one-half of that time was passed in this loathsome place, in darkness, and with such companions—some idea may be formed of what I suffered in this comparatively small portion of my captivity. I have not dwelt upon the miseries which, in addition to those inflicted on all my companions, were peculiarly my own; but I can sincerely say, that not for a Dukedom would I pass such another four months.

We had, however, now and then, a little fun; one of the most prolific sources of which was the exquisite power of mimicry possessed by a diminutive sickly-looking youth. The second overseer was an Irishman, who not only spoke an unusually broad brogue, but exhibited many ludicrous national characteristics. These were caught with the truth of a mirror (only adding a little interest) by our humorous companion; and the object of his ridicule never appeared in sight but an ill-suppressed burst of laughter was heard at his expense. The clever young rogue became an object of even more fear than aversion to our overseer; who would walk half round the prison and back again, rather than encounter his terrible foe.

In the course of the voyage, I took every opportunity of informing myself, as far as possible, of the history and character of my companions, both from themselves and their fellow convicts. No mixed society of free and unconvicted persons could well present greater variety, both morally and intellectually, than these men. There was Dick Pearson, a man of middle age who, though he called himself a sailor, was quite a specimen of the transported convict. He had lived, even from boyhood, by highway robbery, burglary, and other offences of a most daring character. He had been convicted fifteen times, and had already served one penalty of seven years transportation. There was scarcely a known crime in which this man was not adept, or a prison within twenty miles of the metropolis of which he had not been an occupant. To obtain as full an insight as possible into the criminal mind, to judge how far there was any hope of reclaiming such men, and what was most likely to lead to reform, I frequently conversed with Dick and others of his class. In exchange, he asked me a variety of questions upon geography—a kind of curiosity which, as I have already stated, was regarded with much suspicion by the authorities. Indeed, among the convicts, he made no secret that his object was to obtain such information as might be useful to them, if they succeeded in his favourite project of seizing the ship. That he was capable of putting into execution such a design, subsequent events at Norfolk Island sufficiently proved. Upon one occasion, Dick ventured to hint the great possibility of a successful mutiny, as he knew that it would be supported by several of the sailors, and even by some of the military guard; which latter statement was, I am afraid, true. I pointed out to him the preparations which had been made to resist such an attempt, the small chance of victory, the increased suffering which would be entailed upon all the prisoners in case of failure, and that even success could only be purchased by much bloodshed on both sides. This, he said, he considered would be fully justified to obtain their liberty; the faintest hope of which, he thought, well worth the peril of their lives. The attempt to escape at Symon's Bay was planned by him; and subsequently, on landing, he was the ringleader of a more serious and desperate conspiracy for effecting the escape of a large body of the prisoners from Norfolk Island.

How different a character was poor, meek, good-hearted Stoven! He was about fifty years old, and had been for many years a respectable stockbroker. Being unfortunate in some speculations into which he was drawn, he applied himself to that last refuge of the intelligent destitute—the business of a schoolmaster—the profits of which were never adequate to support his large family in decency. In emergencies he had been in the habit of applying to his brother—a wealthy member of one of the learned professions—who occasionally assisted him. On his last application for an advance of five pounds, the brother was unfortunately absent from England; and Stoven, goaded by the sufferings of his family, unhappily conceived the idea of forging his brother's acceptance for the amount of which he had asked the loan; intending, as he assured me, to acquaint his brother of it, persuading himself that he would forgive him and provide for the payment, if he should himself be unable to do so. His moderation, however, was his destruction; for the bill fell into the hands of a gentleman who knew his brother, and expressed his surprise at seeing an acceptance of his in circulation for so insignificant a sum. The brother naturally denied having put his name to any such bill. Inquiries were made, and he was compelled to give evidence against his own brother, to consign him to convict infamy, and, as it proved, to death. He died a victim to the privations and misery of the voyage.

Then we had one of the Rebeccaites.[13] He had been a small farmer in South Wales, and had taken a prominent part in the practical resistance to the turnpike extortion; against which he and his neighbours had petitioned

---

[13] Rebeccaites: related to the Rebecca riots that occurred in South Wales 1842–44 (and so-called as many rioters were disguised as women). The protests were against toll charges on public roads. They were in fact, more a marker of general unrest following the Poor Law Amendment Act of 1834 making poor relief harder to get.

and protested in vain. It has been said that a man cannot unknowingly commit a crime. In a moral sense, at least, this is true; and Morgan, so far from being cognisant of crime, I have no doubt, firmly believed he was discharging his duty to himself and his neighbours. Throughout the voyage, and subsequently in Norfolk Island, the conduct of this man—and of some others of his countrymen (with the exception of one man, a desperate ruffian), who, for a similar offence, were suffering with him—was sufficient to show that they were the unlikeliest of men to be guilty of a moral crime. Dick Pearson, poor Stoven, and Morgan, who may be considered as types of classes aboard, were all members of one mess, enduring the same sufferings (if Dick, hardened as he was, suffered at all), and all with the same sentence of seven years transportation.

Considering our miserable plight as to clothing, food, and everything else, it might be supposed that the thievish propensities of the men must, perforce, have remained in abeyance. Not a day or night, however, passed without some robbery. The worst of them seemed to take a delight in 'keeping their hands in,' no matter how contemptible the prize might be. Knives being forbidden, fragments of tin plates, to serve roughly the purpose of cutting, were eagerly sought for. As I have mentioned, a tin pint pot was delivered to every prisoner at the commencement of the voyage, which served to receive his cocoa, as well as his pea-soup. I had not been at sea a couple of days when I found that mine had been changed. But, as they were scarcely distinguishable one from the other, I gave the new-comer a thorough cleaning, and adopted it in lieu of my own. The very next day, however, a man sidled up to my mess, and suddenly clapping his hand upon the pot, exclaimed, 'Halloa! what are you a-doing with my tin pot?' 'How do you know it is yours?' I inquired. 'There's my mark at the side,' he replied, 'and there should be a round O at the bottom.' I turned it up; and, seeing the mark of identity referred to, felt bound to surrender it. The pot was received with an appearance of indignation, and I was treated as if I had attempted to do a dirty trick, and advised 'not to try that game on again.' My messmates chuckled at the scene; and it was subsequently explained to me that this trick of exchanging was a common trick amongst prisoners. I suffered much inconvenience in consequence for several days; and, for want of my pot to receive them, was deprived of my rations of cocoa, tea and soup. At length I got another; for, happening to mention the trick which had been played me to one of the prisoners, a rough fellow with a most ferocious cast of countenance, he insisted upon my taking his, saying he would try to get the use of his messmates', and reminding me that I had written a letter for him at Woolwich—a circumstance which it is not remarkable that I had forgotten, as I had written at least fifty, while in the river. I had, indeed, frequent proofs that a kindness is sometimes long remembered, and often gratefully requited, by even the worst of criminals.

Towards the end of our voyage, and when about three hundred miles from Norfolk Island, we encountered a terrific storm. The Pacific is like Othello's mind, 'not easily moved; but, being wrought, vexed in the extreme.' For two or three days, it had presented an appearance little in accordance with its name; and, on this night, the storm increased to a hurricane. During the whole night the hatches were fastened down, and we could do nothing but lie and listen to the frequent breaking and long roll of the thunder, the rushing of water over the decks, and the terrific howling of the wind in the rigging. Nothing could be more helpless than our condition in the event of any disaster to the ship. A compact mass of human life closed; fastened down; the narrow outlet strongly barred. We were perfectly helpless. We could hear the din of the sailors running to and fro; and in the intervals of the thunder, their responsive 'Aye, aye, Sir,' to the orders of their captain. At every plunge of the vessel, all seemed to wait in breathless expectation that it was about to founder; but again and again we rose, and the lightning flashing through our tiny portholes, showed distinctly every object in the prison. It was curious to observe the effect of terror upon some of the most hardened of my companions. The most noisy were silent then. Some, who at other times were accustomed to hold in contempt a more civilised mind, asked me—with a tone of civility which I had never experienced from them before—my opinion upon our situation. Men, who were perhaps in action the most daring, finding no resource in their own minds in that terrible and helpless state, appealed to me—as to an oracle—as to 'whether we should go to the bottom;' to which, of course, I could only reply, that in comparison with the number of safe voyages, shipwrecks were extremely rare, and that we were in the hands of a skilful captain.

Our near approach to Norfolk Island was regarded with different feelings by the men. The greater part, who detested regular labour above all things, would, I think, have preferred to spend the rest of their 'lagging'[14] aboard the ship. For my own part, I had an unspeakable desire to leave it; hoping that whatever fresh sufferings might await me, I should at least be placed in less close contiguity with the rest of the prisoners.—At length, after a voyage of four calendar months, we came in sight of our place of captivity. We first saw Nepean Island, which at a distance had an extremely hard and repulsive appearance; but, as the main island came to view, the magnificent Norfolk Island pine trees had an imposing and pleasing aspect. Here and there we had glimpses of the richly wooded slopes which adorn all the islands of the Pacific.

There being no harbour, we lay off about a mile from the coral reefs, the captain exchanging signals with the shore; shortly after which a boat came alongside, rowed by prisoners. We were conveyed ashore under a guard of soldiers in each boat. It was remarkable that after a voyage of seventeen thousand miles, several of my companions were, in this passage of about a mile from the ship to the shore, sea-sick. This was doubtless owing to the new motion of the boat. True to their instincts, they continued to rob one another to the last. One prisoner had a pair of Wellington boots stolen from him in the boat; having on his way to the shore taken them off for some purpose. They were purloined by two other prisoners, who had shared the plunder between them, each being discovered with an odd boot (much too small to be of any use to him) concealed in his trowsers, which having been selected with that disregard for the dimensions of the wearer already mentioned, afforded him ample space for the concealment of any booty of the kind. Two of the guard also complained that they had been robbed of 'sticks' of tobacco.

---

[14] Lagging: term of imprisonment.

On the morning of our landing, a calm had succeeded the storm. The cloudless sky had a brilliant hue known only in that delightful parallel of latitude, which borders on a tropical climate. I felt cheered by the sight of land, and by the healthful breezes which fanned us as we left the ship. I was prepared to meet great hardships; but I did not expect the horrors which awaited me. In happy ignorance, my feelings were rather of an agreeable kind as I first set foot on that paradise; which, changed by the wickedness of man, has been since termed, 'The Ocean Hell.'

7
Transported for Life [Part Two]
William Moy Thomas

Details Barber's imprisonment on Norfolk Island; his release and subsequent transfer
to Van Diemen's Land. It outlines his journey to Sydney and his final return to
England.
Volume: 5 Number: 124 Pages: 482–89
Date: August 7, 1852
Fee: 5 pounds 5 shillings for 13 ½ Columns.

As I stood upon the beach, waiting for the remainder of the prisoners from
the ship, and musing upon the strange destiny which had cast me among
such companions, I could not help comparing my position, society, and
prospects with those of that day twelve months. It was the 9th of November,
the day of the great City festival, and I remembered well the 9th of November
previously, a different kind of day to that bright cloudless morning. I was
then enjoying a large income, with the brightest prospects. What a catalogue
of ills I had suffered in those twelve months! The wreck of all that I possessed
in the world; the estrangement of friends, the severance from those I dearly
loved, imprisonment in three different dungeons, branded with all but a
capital crime, transported for life to the worst of all penal settlements.

As the precise time of our arrival could not of course be previously
known, no preparations had been made to receive us. The commissariat
issues had already been made for that day, and thus, although we landed in
the morning, we got nothing to eat till the next day. We were compelled to
sleep on the floor of a granary; a bundle of blankets were thrown in to us, for
which there was an immediate struggle, some getting two, others none at all.
Next morning we were summoned by five o'clock, and taken down to bathe

in a bay near the landing-place. This done, we had our breakfast—a dish of hominy, or boiled Indian corn. It was poor and insipid, but not disagreeable. As we were all considerably exhausted by a four months' voyage, a little time was necessary to make arrangements for setting us to work; we were allowed two days' rest, preparatory to entering upon our island labours. During this time, we were permitted to walk about the settlement and make ourselves acquainted with the establishments. The barracks for the prisoners were immediately fronting the sea; those of the military guard, consisting of two hundred men and officers, being about a quarter of a mile in the rear. On a pleasant elevation overlooking the settlement, was Government House, the residence of the civil commandant; and in the immediate neighbourhood were about a dozen villas, the residences of the chaplain, the engineer, and other civil officers. On the first day, we were all drawn up in the barrack square and inspected by the civil commandant, accompanied by the medical superintendent who had charge of us on our voyage. The commandant, addressing us, asked, 'Has any man any complaint to make of the doctor?' but no complaint was made. The agricultural labourers were sent to a station called Longridge, about two miles inland, the rest being retained in the settlement. When the commandant and the medical superintendent retired, the chaplain paid us a visit. He was an intelligent, and, as I subsequently found, most benevolent man.

In the course of the two days' rest, I had an opportunity of inspecting the dormitories of the prisoners, and other parts of the establishment. I saw a body of men called the 'chain gang.' These were incorrigible offenders. Their legs were chained together, so that as they went to and fro to their work, they could step but a few inches at a time. Their appearance was abject in the extreme. The police were a smart-looking set of fellows, selected from the finest-looking men among the prisoners, very clean, and wearing striped shirts, blue jackets, and white duck trowsers, with leathern belts, and hats made from the cabbage-tree, which flourished on the Island, strips of which, woven and plaited, looked like straw. The police, however, either from negligence or connivance, or perhaps from sympathy with the prisoners, being themselves convicts, were very inefficient; for robberies were constantly committed in open day, in the heart of the settlement.

On my visit to the gaol, I had opportunities of observing some remarkable features in the conduct of that establishment. I was surprised at witnessing a pitched battle in the courtyard, under the eye of the governor of the gaol. Two men were brought out of the same cell; their chains were knocked off, and they had a set pugilistic encounter, until one of them avowing himself beaten, their chains were put on again, and they retired together into their cell. I was much struck with this novel feature in prison discipline, and ventured to ask the gaoler about it. He said, 'Oh! they've been quarrelling for some time, and I thought it better they should fight it out.' Shortly after, the dinners were taken round to the prisoners; and as the wardsman took the supply to each cell, he was vigilantly guarded by two soldiers with bayonets fixed, and the food was hastily and stealthily thrust in at the door, apparently with more alarm than the keeper of Wombwell's menagerie ever felt in feeding the most ferocious of his wild beasts. I found, upon inquiry, that these precautions were by no means superfluous, instances having occurred of most savage assaults upon the wardsmen by unhappy wretches, who had been rendered almost maniacs by sentences of solitary imprisonment for life in chains.

The sudden change from the ship ration to that of the Island, of which the hominy was the chief feature, gave at least a third of our men, myself included, an attack of dysentery, and I was thereby introduced to the medical superintendent of the Island, an able and humane man. Those who were well enough to work were all employed, either in trade, in husbandry, or as writers, according to their previous pursuits and qualifications, although access by convicts to the records of the Island was expressly forbidden by a regulation of the Home Government. I, with several others, was compelled to go into the hospital, where one of our party, an athletic Sussex farming man, died of the epidemic superinduced by the hominy. The illness of the men was attributed by some to the change of climate, but that theory was negatived by the fact that not one of the free officers, who landed with us, suffered at all. It is beyond doubt that dysentery and death were in numerous instances solely attributable to the diet.˜

The hospital was a low stone building close to the sea. Into the ward in which I lay, ten low pallets had been crammed with difficulty, and the heat was excessive; but there was a stillness about the place, and a gentle manner with my sick companions, subdued by suffering, which were strange after the noise and coarse brutality to which I had been so long accustomed. At night-time a cooler air came through the half-opened window, and it was a pleasure to lie awake and listen to the rolling of the sea upon the beach. But, as might be expected, there was little there to soothe the sufferer in the weariness of long sickness, much less to strengthen his soul in that last moment which is so terrible in its mystery even for the wisest and the best. Many of the most daring of the convicts have wrung a kind of respect from those over them by the terror of their vengeance—some ruffians indeed, to my knowledge, have even struck those high in command, and been suffered to go unpunished; but the sick and helpless could expect little consideration. Several deaths occurred while I was there, and the sense of the suffering around me depressed my spirits and retarded my convalescence.

How different was this from all that I had previously known and associated with the idea of the sick-bed, the hushed and darkened room where you alone are ill, and every one about you is in good health, and you are the sole object of their pity and attention! Feverish and weary with long lying on my hard bed, the knowledge that there were many about me whose sufferings were greater than mine, instead of consoling me, seemed to shut me out from all compassion, and to make my misery still more unendurable. Nothing was there to remind me that sickness was an exceptional state, no token of health or cheerfulness which I too might hope one day to regain;— the greatest wretchedness of that wretched spot brought together where I lay, all life seemed to me sickly and overshadowed with death. And where were they who, the last time I had been ill, had sought by a hundred ways to make my sufferings lighter? Whose cares, even when they gave me no relief, brought still a consolation in the kindly feeling which they showed? Did they still believe in my innocence in spite of all that had been brought against me? To some of those beside me, well-nigh worn out with pain, the approach of death, I thought, must seem an unaccustomed blessing: but to me how terrible was the thought of dying in that place!˜

There were those in England for whose sakes, and on account of the sorrow and shame which my conviction had brought upon them, I prayed fervently to be spared for that day when I could make my innocence clear. For although with my last breath I had asserted the injustice of my sentence, in language so strong that any doubts which they might hold would have been dispelled, who was there to communicate the last words of a dying convict to his friends on the other side of the globe? It was this thought which urged me to obtain ink and paper, which I did with much difficulty, in order to write a complete history and explanation of my case, in the hope of finding means of forwarding it to England. This task, though accomplished with great difficulty, was the principle which, I believe, alone sustained me in that miserable place. Ill as I was, I never failed to avail myself of an opportunity for continuing my task, sometimes hurriedly concealing my manuscript under the bed-clothes at the sound of a footstep, with an anxious fear lest some one would deprive me of my papers, or in a moment destroy the fruit of my labours; until at length one day I saw it finished. I have not forgotten how joyfully I wrote the last sheet. That day I hid the whole of the manuscript under my pillow, and slept a sweeter and a longer sleep than I had known since I left England.

The relief afforded by the change of rations, aided by proper medicines, enabled me in about a month to leave that scene of misery and death. I was, however, still in a very weakly condition, and as the doctor reported me unfit for severe physical labour, and it was customary to allow the superintendents of different divisions of convicts the services as writers of such of them as had been well educated, and two or three of our party had been so employed, I rejoiced to find that several applications were now made for my services. For reasons not then known to me, these applications were refused, and I had the misfortune to be appointed 'Wardsman'; this was by far the most loathsome, perilous, and unhealthy occupation on the Island. Its duties were to preserve order in a dormitory of two hundred criminals, many of whom, as subsequent events showed, would not scruple to take the life of an individual who, like myself, was at once their drudge and their overseer. Locked in with these ruffians, from seven in the evening until six o'clock on the following morning, my task was then to cleanse and purify their dormitory for their reception and accommodation the next night. The disgusting details of the labour thus selected for me, I will not go into.˜

The doctor pointed out various labours besides that of writer, such as hut-keeper, bag-mender, &c., suited to me, and protested in vain against the invidious cruelty to which I was subjected. The men being shut in the ward about ten or twelve hours every night, they did not, of course, sleep all the time. To amuse themselves in the darkness they would form little groups to listen to one of their number narrating his exploits. Others who had nothing exciting to tell in this way were driven to relate little stories, often of the most childish kind. It was a strange thing, and full of matter for reflection, to hear men, in whose rough tones I sometimes recognised some of the most stolid and hardened of the prisoners, gravely narrating an imperfectly remembered version of such childish stories as 'Jack the Giant Killer,' for the amusement of their companions, who, with equal gravity, would correct him from their own recollections, or enter into a ridiculous discussion on some of the facts. Familiar as they were with crime—in all that concerned book-lore they were but children, and when they found themselves driven to seek some amusement for the mind, the old nursery tales—the fact of their knowing which, I thought, showed that in infancy, at least, some one had regarded them with affection—were all that they could find. Seeing this, I tried the experiment of some stories from English and Roman History, to which they listened with eager attention, urging me to repeat and extend my narratives.

When I had been on the Island about ten weeks, a most desperate attempt at escape was made by a party of prisoners. The ship in which we performed our voyage had since been to Sydney, and returned with provisions and troops. A gang of prisoners, about twenty in number, had been employed as a boat's crew to assist in bringing the stores as well as the troops from the ship. Whilst engaged in this labour, a well-organised conspiracy was formed to effect their escape, and which nearly succeeded. For this purpose, provisions and other requisites had been got together—probably spared from their own messes, or contributed by other convicts to whom they had communicated their intentions. Everything was kept a profound secret; for it is a remarkable fact that, although political conspiracies, as we are taught by history, are almost invariably brought to light by the treachery or cowardice of one of the confederates, plots among convicts are rarely divulged even by those who, having no interest in the venture, have been accidentally made privy to it.

These provisions they found opportunities of burying in the sands of the sea-shore, at a place called Windmill Point, about half-a-mile distant. There being no harbour, the vessel lay at about a mile from the beach. All being prepared, one morning the boat left the shore as usual, with a crew consisting of twelve prisoners, a coxswain, and three soldiers with pistols loaded. About half way to the ship, the whole of the prisoners, upon some signal from their ringleader, rose simultaneously, and flung themselves upon the coxswain and guard before they had time to fire. The coxswain was instantly secured and bound; but the soldiers were either thrown into the sea, or in their fright leaped overboard. The head of the gang, Dick Pearson, a daring fellow who had been a seaman and who aided the escape of the man at Symon's Bay, seized the helm and directed the boat towards the headland, called Windmill Point, to take in their supplies and some of their confederates. These latter, however, had been detained by some accidental circumstances, and the boat was kept lying off until it attracted the attention of some parties on the shore near this point, as well as of the captain of the ship.

The military were immediately summoned to the spot. Signs were made to them to ship their oars in token of surrender, but Dick Pearson was not the man to yield, or to allow the others to give way to their fears. They were within half musket-shot from the shore, but he, sitting still at the helm coolly steering the boat, ordered them, in a voice that could be heard from the shore, to pull for their lives. The soldiers levelled, the word was given to fire, and immediately a line of musketry flashed and cracked along the beach. When the smoke cleared away, however, the soldiers being armed with the good old British musket, the men were still seen rowing in the boat, their daring leader sitting still at the helm apparently untouched; and, although several volleys were discharged before they were completely out of gunshot range, not one of the party was struck. The mutineers, although they had not been able to secure their provisions, put out to sea with all speed. It was well known among the convicts that such attempts have almost invariably failed; and in all cases have been attended with privations, in comparison with which, what they endured on the island were insignificant. But the passion for liberty is no mere flourish of poets and orators. Something more than a consideration of the comparative material enjoyments of the one and the other state, is at the bottom of that longing to be free, which will sometimes induce even those to whom every generous sentiment would seem to be unknown, to incur risks disproportioned to the utmost increase of personal comfort which they can expect to gain. The position of many on the Island, in comparison with their previous life, could not have been extremely irksome; but the sense of restraint is continually with them, becoming, at last, almost insupportable. It is, indeed, no problem to me that these men, in spite of the preparations for retaking them, which they could see on shore and aboard the vessel and which made their escape hopeless, continued to strain every muscle for their miserable chance of getting out on the wide ocean, without sail, compass, or provisions. The captain, observing their motions and having the wind in his favour, effectually hemmed them in, and they were compelled to surrender. Knowing the general character of the men, and the feeling which animates them, I do not doubt that if they had had any arms they would even then have made a desperate resistance; and of this the records of attempts to escape from the Island afford abundant instances. A lengthened investigation subsequently took place. The soldiers swore that they were seized upon and violently flung overboard; the prisoners, on the other hand, protested that they leaped into the sea in their fright, or accidentally fell over in the struggle.

In favour of the latter view there was a strong circumstance, and which showed so much humanity as to create great doubt whether they were fairly chargeable with the cruelty of purchasing their own liberty, with the sacrifice of the lives of the guard. The men, seeing the soldiers struggling in the water, threw to them one of the oars, to which they clung until they were picked up by a boat from the shore. It was of course a very important question, whether the mutineers had been merely guilty of an attempt to escape, or whether to that was added the crime of an attempt of murder. The men were afterwards tried by a jury of five military officers; when the guard, uncatechised,[1] echoed of course the statements in their depositions; and the accused were all convicted and condemned to death. This sentence would, I feel sure, have

---

[1]Uncatechised: one who has received little or no religious education.

been carried into effect, but for the interposition of the chaplain. As it was, their original sentences were extended to transportation for life.

It was during my detention in the Island that the famous massacre, headed by Westwood, *alias* Jacky Jacky, already described in a previous number of *Household Words*,[2] took place. One of the principal causes which led to that fearful outbreak was the stoppage of the daily allowance of two pounds of potatoes, which, from the saltiness of the beef, were in that hot climate almost absolutely necessary. Upon the failure of the potato crop, an equivalent for these two pounds of sweet potatoes was sought, and it was at length determined by the authorities that two ounces of raw salt pork, being exactly similar in money value, should be given as a substitute. The official report says: 'This has created much dissatisfaction among the men generally, from the very small quantity, which could, with due regard to the public purse, be apportioned: and so difficult has it been to make the men comprehend the equity of such an equivalent, that a large number for a long time refused to receive it, in the hope that some other substitute would ultimately be granted them.' The substitution of two ounces of pork for two pounds of potatoes was an exasperating mockery, which the men bore with patience until the sudden seizure of all their pots and cooking utensils, when an outbreak ensued, resulting in a fearful loss of life.

Fourteen men, in all, were tried by special commission for the Jacky Jacky massacre. An eye-witness of the proceedings on the trial states that the majority manifested no contrition for their offence. Some laughed and jested; others browbeat witnesses in a style quite professional, and, I presume, acquired in a long experience of courts of justice in England. One addressed the Court at considerable length, after having cleverly examined the witnesses, speaking fluently and well, enumerating all the weak points in the evidence against him, and noting every discrepancy in the facts. This man was more deeply implicated than any, except Westwood. Another, an Irish lad of scarce twenty years of age, began his defence by calling a witness, whom, after a careful personal scrutiny, he dismissed without a question, professing

---

[2] See also, 'Norfolk Island' [*Household Words*, 10 April 1852, No. 107, pp. 73–77; see also p. 39 in this volume].

'not to like the look of the fellow.' Having called another witness, who described himself as a 'scourger or flagellator,'[3] much merriment ensued among the prisoners, and the Irish lad finally joked him out of the witness-box, and called another, with whom the following dialogue took place:—

Prisoner: You're Darker, I believe?

Witness: I am.

Prisoner: You've an extensive acquaintance on the island?

Witness: I know the men on the settlement mostly.

Prisoner: Divil doubt ye! It's the big rogues is best known. Now, Darker, tell me. Didn't ye some months ago say to a man on this island, that you had so much villainy in yir head, that it was a-busting out at yir ears?

Here the judge's patience was exhausted, although such scenes are common on such occasions, and the witness was ordered to stand down. Twelve were found guilty. On hearing their sentences they became extremely violent, cursing the prosecutor and all connected with the trial. Westwood alone was calm and orderly. At the conclusion of the sentence he rose, and in a calm, unbroken voice addressed the Court. He seemed contrite, but had lost none of that coolness and air of resolution, which had characterised him throughout. He expressed deep sorrow for his share in the massacre, sensible that he could say but little in extenuation of it. He expected to suffer, and was content to die, but regretted that innocent men should be involved in the punishment. It was observed, however, that he did not mention any names. He went on to say that he entered life with a kindly feeling towards his fellow-men, which had been changed into misanthropy by harsh treatment, fraud, and cruelty. 'Since childhood,' he exclaimed, 'I have never known what kindness was. I have struggled for liberty, and have robbed, when in the bush, to supply the cravings of nature but I never raised my hand against a fellow-creature till the present time.' He complained bitterly of the harsh treatment he had received, not at Norfolk Island, but previously in Van Dieman's Land. It was said by an officer on the Island that, in his case, there was some ground for the complaint; for he had heard that an act of brutality on the part of an overseer was the occasion of Westwood's absconding and

---

[3] Scourger or flagellator: one who whips or flogs for punishment.

taking to those courses, which now, at the age of twenty-six, brought him to an ignominious end.

The twelve were hanged, with five others, a few days afterwards; the office of executioner being filled by two convicts who volunteered their services. There were upwards of twenty candidates for the appointment. One of the two men selected stated, in his written application, that having been a notorious offender and now deeply penitent for his past misconduct, he 'hoped to be permitted to retrieve his character by serving the Government on the present occasion.'

I continued at my disgusting employment of wardsman for sixteen months, only interrupted by the frequent illnesses and returns to the hospital which it produced. It was not until the good chaplain, who was at my pallet-side every day, believed me to be dying, that the doctor's recommendation was partially complied with. I was removed to the Cascades—a more salubrious part of the Island; though even there I was ordered to perform the very duties which had so repeatedly brought me to the brink of the grave. The change of air, however, had a beneficial effect, but, I had no sooner recovered my strength, than I was ordered back, and sent to field labour in a heavy gang, with a doubly convicted felon for my overseer—notorious for his severity, and for the irritating and frivolous accusations he constantly made against the twenty-four men committed to his control; either of whom he could at any moment get flogged or imprisoned upon his unsupported testimony. Fortunately I did not incur his displeasure.

Covered with dirt, weakened from insufficient food; sometimes drenched with rain, at others, standing up to my knees in slush, and under a broiling sun that made the mud steam around me, I continued at this horrible labour for three months, when a vacancy occurred in a writership, which it was found difficult to fill, and the commandant was at length compelled to yield to a pressing application for my services. I was, therefore, at length permitted to lay aside the hoe for the pen; but even in this improved condition, I had the same rations, and was at the desk from five in the morning until nine at night; and when my appetite for the coarse food which I had been able to eat while toiling in the open air was destroyed by the close sedentary confinement, and my superintendent asked for me the indulgence of a little milk daily, in lieu of the salt meat which I could not eat, it was refused.

Among the many remarkable prisoners in the island, by no means the least so was my predecessor in this writership. He was a native of Bengal, where he had received an excellent education; was a fine classic, and spoke several modern languages fluently. He had acquired considerable distinction in the British legion in Spain. Upon his return to England he fell into dissipated and extravagant habits, to support which he forged bills of exchange on a British nobleman, whose acquaintance he had made. He was a good-looking but delicate man, and fond of comparing himself with Abd-el-Kader,[4] to whose portraits he bore a strong resemblance.

We had prisoners from every part of the British dominions, and, indeed, from almost every part of the world. Besides English, Irish, Scotch, Frenchmen, Italians, and Germans, there were Chinamen from Hong Kong, Aborigines from New Holland, West Indian Blacks, Greeks, Caffres [Kaffirs], and Malays. Among these were soldiers, for desertion, idiots, madmen, boys of seventeen, and old men of eighty. All these were indiscriminately herded together, without reference to age, crime, nation, or any other distinction.

Upon the whole, the conduct of the prisoners to me was extremely kind. Thus, when it was my turn to carry a bundle of heavy hoes to the field, they would frequently insist upon relieving me of the load. Upon one occasion, whilst drawing water from a deep well, my straw hat (which had been ordered by the doctor) fell to the bottom; upon which, one of the men, whom I scarcely knew, immediately caught hold of the chain, and insisted upon descending to fetch it. It was in vain I entreated him not to incur such a risk merely for a hat, and pointed out the insecurity of the chain. He went down, and I stood watching with trembling anxiety at the top. At length, to my unspeakable relief, he was wound up again; when he handed me the hat, saying, 'One good turn deserves another.' What the good turn may have been that I had done him, I never had the slightest idea.

---

[4] Abd-el-Kader: Algerian military and religious leader who led a struggle against the French 1840–46.

Nothing, however, could induce them to resist the temptation of thieving. They soon stole my shoes while I was asleep. When a humane officer observed me working at the water-cart barefoot, in a heavy rain, he sent me a pair of his own boots. The untiring kindness of the young man convicted of forgery, whose despair and sufferings on board ship I have already described, I shall ever remember with the deepest gratitude. Frequently, when he found me sinking under my heavy trials, he would insist upon sharing my task. It was the happiest moment of my life upon the Island, when an opportunity presented itself of making him some return. He had from the first been employed as chief writer in an office, and discharged his duties in a most exemplary manner for eighteen months, when a few sticks of tobacco were found concealed in the clothes of a fellow clerk; and my friend was suspected of being a party to its introduction into the office. Dishonesty was not imputed to either of them; but the use of tobacco, or the traffic in it, was a grave offence. They were, accordingly, for the first time, both sent into the field to work in a broiling sun in the gullies. After a few days I successfully employed some influence which I had now acquired, and got my friend again placed in an office, where he remained.

Wretched as my condition was here, it was not without its agreeable and even happy moments. As soon as my case had become better known by the investigations which took place, sympathy was expressed towards me, not only by the worthy chaplain, but by the civil and military officers generally. They entered into conversation with me in the course of their walks and rides, whether they found me in the ward, at the stone-heap, in the plough-field, or at the desk. Anxious to be as useful as possible, I every evening in the week, as well as morning and afternoon on Sundays, taught in the schools and distributed books among the men. These duties brought me into frequent communication with the chaplain, who would sometimes detain me a whole evening. In the charm of his refined society and instructive conversation, I have, for the time, forgotten my sad condition. Often, when the last bell announced the moment for locking up for the night, I seemed to be rudely awakened from some pleasant dream. What a change of scene and of company, from the chaplain and his library, to the convicts and their loathsome hut!

My duties now frequently took me to various parts of the Island, affording me opportunities of remarking on its beauties. Its entire length is about ten miles; its breadth about seven. It is evidently of recent volcanic origin. It is beautifully diversified by hills and valleys, and the sea is in sight from almost every part. For the free inhabitants who do not have to labour in the heat of the day, the climate is luxurious—a delicious sea-breeze playing constantly over the Island. Peaches, guavas, grapes, bananas, and other fruits grow everywhere. In the gardens of the officers, pomegranates, loquats, and other delicious fruits were in great perfection. In winter, peas, cabbages, and other European vegetables are produced in abundance.

The coast is everywhere indented with bays and inlets. In one of these retired nooks I have sometimes enjoyed a bath which a prince might have envied. The woods were filled with parrots and other birds of magnificent plumage; but their notes were most monotonous. The birds of the Pacific isles have no song. The nights in Norfolk Island are more beautiful than a European can imagine. The moon gives a light by which a newspaper may be read with ease. The air is generally clear; and during the writership, when I had a hut to myself in the midst of a large garden, I have frequently at dead of night left my hammock and walked about the garden, with no other clothing than my night-dress, without experiencing the slightest ill effect.

We had but one storm during my stay there, but that was terrific. Such rain! it came down rather in sheets than in drops; and the thunder seemed to shake the very island. Snow had not been seen for many years. None of the trees are deciduous, and the pasture-lands there present the appearance of a rich green velvet. Mount Pitt, a thousand feet above the level of the sea, is crowned with trees of the richest foliage and every variety of tint. Conspicuous amongst them rises the graceful Norfolk Island pine. The lanes in many parts of the Island are lined on each side by lemon trees, meeting overhead, and hung with the golden fruit, forming a fragrant bower miles in length. The harbour of Sydney is highly picturesque; Ceylon is magnificent in scenery; and there are parts of Van Dieman's Land of great beauty; but Norfolk Island is the loveliest spot I ever beheld. How strange, I have often thought, that such a Paradise should be the chosen abode of the refuse of criminals, doubly and trebly sifted.

I had passed two years and six months on the Island when news arrived, that, in consequence of representations made to the home authorities of the abominations and misgovernment in that settlement, the establishment was to be broken up; and I was removed with three hundred other prisoners to Van Dieman's Land.

For more than three years I had now been deprived of my liberty. 'Hope deferred' had, long since, made my heart sick. Letters and statements, which I had myself written and despatched to England under the greatest difficulties, while labouring in the fields, and while sick in the hospital, had served to keep alive my hopes; and it was well for me, perhaps, when after fixing the time that must elapse before a reply could be returned, and marking anxiously the months as they rolled away, I eagerly watched for the arrival of a vessel in the harbour, that I was ignorant of the fact that scarcely one of these appeals ever reached its destination, and that one upon which I had most relied, addressed by the chaplain of the Island to the first Minister of the Crown, had got no further than Hobart Town. At length, however, the noble exertions of a gentleman who had been unceasing in his inquiries into every fact connected with my case were successful. About a week after my removal to Van Dieman's Land, I received the intelligence that a conditional 'pardon' had arrived, giving me liberty, though without permission to land in England.

The superintendent, who communicated to me this news, said, 'You must give me your prison clothing, and proceed to Hobart Town, where you will receive the necessary document.' Having no clothes of my own, or any money or friends to assist me in that part, I asked what clothes would be given or lent me to travel in. To this he merely replied, 'I have no orders about that.' The principal communication with Hobart Town was by water, but as the pardon was unaccompanied by any authority for a free passage, I was unable to obtain one. By land it was about ninety miles, through an almost untrodden region—a gum tree wilderness—without for the greater part any roads, except a slight kind of sheep track, at many places quite effaced by heavy rains; but I was compelled to go, and for aught that the Government provided me, under such extraordinary circumstances, I might have wandered to Hobart Town naked and without food. My miserable fellow prisoners however had more compassion, and clubbed together such few odd articles of wearing apparel as they happened to possess; and the superintendent and the religious instructor kindly eked out the charity of those whose fellow captive I had so long been, to enable me to set out upon my journey—a wandering mendicant round the earth—having the fixed resolve to proceed to Paris, a distance of twenty thousand miles, there to renew my struggle for that justice which I knew must be the result of a re-examination of the facts of my case. I sometimes travelled thirty miles of that weary, though welcome journey, without seeing a human being from whom to inquire my way. Knowing, however, the position of Hobart Town, the sun served as my compass by day and the stars by night. My course sometimes lay along the sea-coast; but oftener deep in the woods, on emerging from which, the scenery was often extremely beautiful. After crossing mountains and fording streams, and sleeping occasionally in the shade of a tree, in three days and three nights I reached my destination. Had a stage harlequin suddenly made his appearance, he could scarcely have attracted more attention than I did, in my motley, ill-fitting suit. I was, however, soon metamorphosed, being most kindly received by the chaplain and the Judge of Assize who had known me in my captivity.

After a brief stay at Hobart Town, aided by subscriptions from the Lieutenant-Governor and other principal inhabitants, I took ship for Sydney. Here my case was fully reviewed and investigated, and I received further and very liberal assistance to prosecute my journey. In fifty days I reached Canton, and in thirty more, Madras. Having letters of introduction to the judges and other persons of distinction there, I was received and entertained with munificent hospitality. For three weeks, while I waited for the steamer to convey me to Suez, I became the guest of one of the chief officers of the Presidency, who appropriated a suite of apartments, bath-room, library, carriage, and two servants, to my especial use. What a charming scene is a dinner-party in India! The very heat is made a source of delight. A feeling of deep repose is in the dusty saloon. The floor, paved with smooth stone, without carpet; the air rendered deliciously cool by passing through wet matting; the eye refreshed by the choicest flowers encircling the doorway and drooping in through the open windows; the guests attired in snow-white dresses of Chinese grass-cloth, more cool and delicate than the finest muslin; the bare-footed native servants, in their white robes and red turbans, gliding noiselessly about; everything reminds you of those Oriental stories which we are earliest taught, and whose scenes, long after floating in the mind, become the elements of dreams. From above the punka[5] kept up an artificial breeze, while ice appeared as plentiful as if we had been regaling ourselves on the Grands Mulets.[6] What Eastern story could be more strange than those vicissitudes which had finally brought me amid such scenes.

I reached Paris by the overland route *via* Trieste, passing through Southern Germany, and down the Danube and the Rhine, having letters of introduction to eminent persons there. Through them I succeeded in securing the attention of Her Majesty's ambassador to my case; and, after the lapse of six months, I received a free pardon, with a letter from the Secretary of State acknowledging my innocence.

Notes

Following the inquiry into Barber's case a small book was published in Sydney (1847)—*The Case of Mr. W.H. Barber ... convicted in 1844 of a supposed guilty knowledge of certain will forgeries, consisting of his memorial to Sir James Graham and other documents establishing ... his innocence ... with editorial remarks by Archibald Michie.*[7] (See, Nat Library of Aust.FRMF4467).

It documents about twenty six statements and accounts supporting Barber's innocence or lack of wrong doing. The fifty three-page book (in very fine print) contained a two-page preface penned by Archibald Michie, a Sydney lawyer and Magistrate. The book has two pages entitled 'Brief Outline' which may have been written by Michie, and at the end there is a

---

[5] Punka: a large swinging fan made of canvas stretched over a rectangular frame hung from the ceiling.

[6] Grands Mulets: a part of walk on Mt Blanc, France.

[7] Sir Archibald Michie contributed two articles to *Household Words*, (reprinted in this collection: see, Book 1 and Book 4). For more details on Michie, see biographical information on p. 168 in this volume.

section headed 'Observations' (consisting of eight pages) which is not attributed, but may conceivably have been written by him. Mitchie was not a member of the committee involved in reviewing Barber's case (per. com. Paul Livingston, Snr.Reference Librarian—Nat.Lib.Aust).

A Parliamentary enquiry was later established to review Barber's case and its findings of his innocence published in a Select Committee Report in London (1848) (Parliamentary paper 397, 1847–48). The following year (1849) Barber published a book on his experiences (Dickens had a copy in his library).

8
Chip: Transported for Life
W.H. Wills

Follow-up comments to the previous article – "Transported for Life" (Part Two).[1]
Volume: 5 Number: 127 Pages: 566–67
Date: August 28, 1852
Fee: No Fee shown for ¾ Column.

It appears that since the return of the subject of 'Transported for Life' (see pages 455 and 482 of the present volume); some modifications have taken place in the rules applicable to persons banished to the British penal colonies. We are informed that now, no prisoner is sent to Norfolk Island unless he has proved utterly incorrigible during his detention in a less penal settlement. Neither is the sentence of transportation from this country so immediately carried out as formerly. The following are the official regulations in this respect:

'A prisoner under sentence for life, who had passed twelve months in separate confinement, would, by exemplary conduct for five years on public works, become eligible for embarkation.

'Minimum period of detention on public works applicable to prisoners whose conduct is exemplary:

'A prisoner sentenced to 7 years, for a period of 1 year.

Ditto	"	10 '	"	"	1¾	"
Ditto	"	20 '	"	"	4	"
Ditto	"	Life	"	"	5	"

after which they are sent out as holders of tickets of leave.'

---

[1] See p. 72 in this volume.

When a prisoner has conducted himself well during his probation he is furnished with a ticket of leave in the colony to which he may be sent, is allowed to hire himself for wages, to live in a dwelling of his own,—and to such an extent are his privileges carried—that Government even partially defrays the expense of sending out to him his wife and family. The only conditions annexed to his ticket of leave are that he shall be well-conducted, and report himself periodically to the Police Office of the district in which he may reside.

9
The New Colonists of Norfolk Island
Rev. William B Ullathorne

Re-settlement of the people from Pitcairn Island to Norfolk Island. Description of the Island and of the establishment of introduced species of plants. Reprinted from William B. Ullathorne, *The Catholic Mission in Australia,* published first in England in 1836.
Volume: 16 Number: 399 Pages: 476–77
Date: November 14 1857
Fee: Item not in office book for 2 Columns.

The story of the Pitcairn islanders, the descendants of the mutineers of the Bounty, is well known. Having so multiplied that they have outgrown the agricultural resources of Pitcairn Island, they have lately been removed at their own request, at the expense of the British government, to Norfolk Island, a place hitherto only known as a crowded convict settlement—a horror of horrors. The following description is extracted from a pamphlet published by the Roman Catholic Bishop Ullathorne, about twenty years ago. It will be seen that the descendants of Adams are now planted on a fertile soil under a genial sun. We have a right to expect remarkable agricultural and horticultural results from their industry.

'Norfolk Island is one thousand miles from Sydney, about twenty-one miles in circumference, of volcanic origin, and one of the most beautiful spots in the world.

'Rising abruptly on all sides but one from the sea, clustering columns of basalt spring out of the sea, securing at intervals its endurance with the strong architecture of God.

'That one side presents a low sandy level, on which is, or was formerly, situated the penal settlement. It is approachable only by boats, through a narrow bar in the reef of coral, which, visible here, invisibly circles the island.

'The island consists of a series of hills curiously interfolded, the green ridges rising one above another until they reach the craggy sides and crowning summit of Mount Pitt, at the height of three thousand feet above the level of the sea.

Figure 1.5 Sydney Bay, Norfolk Island, to which place a portion of the Pitcairn Islanders are in the course of removal by Malby & Sons. HMS *Herald*, May 1855. Image courtesy of National Library of Australia: nla.pic-an9060932.

'The establishment consists of a spacious quadrangle of buildings for the prisoners, the military barracks, and a series of offices in two ranges. A little further beyond, on a green mound, the mansion of the commandant, with barred windows, guarded by cannon and a pacing sentinel.

'Straying some distance along a footpath, we came upon the cemetery, closed in on three sides by close, thick, melancholy groves of tear-dropping manchineel;[1] the fourth is open to the booming sea. The graves are

---

[1] Manchineel: tropical American tree or shrub.

numerous; most of the tenants have reached their last abode by an untimely end. I myself have witnessed fifteen descents into those houses of mortality: in every one is a hand of blood.

'Passing on by a ledge cut in the cliff that hangs over the resounding shore, we suddenly turn into an amphitheatre of hills, which rise all around until they close in a circle of the blue cloudless heavens above, their sides being thickly clothed with curious wild shrubs, wild flowers, and wild vines. Passing a brawling brook, and long and slowly ascending, we again reach the open varied ground: here a tree-crested mound, there a plantation of pines, and yonder below, descending into the very bowels of the earth, and covered with an intricacy of dark foliage, interluminated with chequers of sun-light, until beyond it opens a receding vista to the blue sea. And now the path closes, so that the sun is almost shut out; whilst giant creepers shoot, twist, and contort themselves upon your path; beautiful lories, parrots, paroquets, and other birds, rich and varied in plumage, spring up at your approach.

'We next reach a valley of exquisite beauty, in the middle of which, where the winding gurgling stream is jagged in its course, spring up a cluster of some eight fern-trees, with a clear, black, mossy stem, from the crown of which shoots out on every side one long arching fern-leaf.

'Ascending again through the dank forest, we meet rising on every side, amongst other strange forest trees, the gigantic pine of Norfolk Island; which, ascending with a clear stem of vast circumference some twelve feet, shoots out a coronal of dark boughs, each in shape like the feathers of the ostrich indefinably prolonged, until rising with clear intervals, horizontal, stage above stage the green, pyramid cuts with its point the blue ether at the height of two hundred feet.

'Through these groves we at length reach the summit of Mount Pitt. Below us lies a wondrous scene in a narrow space—rock, valley, forest, corn-field, islet, alive with purple, crimson, snow-white birds of land and sea, in a light of glowing sunshine framed in the vast expanse of the Pacific Ocean.

'Descending, we take a new path. After awhile, emerging from the deep gloom of the forest, amid glades and openings may be seen the guava and the lemon, the fern and the palmetto, rising to the height of twenty-five feet, and then spreading into a shade of bright broad green fans.

'Then parasite creepers and climbers rise up in columns, shoot over arch after arch, and again descend in every variety of Gothic fantasy—now form a high, long wall, dense, impenetrable; then tumble down in a cascade of green leaves, frothed over with the delicate white convolvulus.

'Our way at length becomes a long vista of lemon-trees, forming overhead an arcade of green, gold, and sunlight. Orange-trees once crowded the island as thickly, but were cut down by a former commandant, as too great a luxury for the convict.

'On the farms, the yellow hulm bends with the fat of corn; in the gardens, by the broad-breasted English oak, grows the delicate cinnamon-tree, the tea, the coffee-shrub, the sugarcane, the banana, with its long weeping streamers and creamy fruit,—the fig. All tropical fruits in perfection; English vegetables of gigantic growth.

'The air is pure, ambient; the sky brilliant. At night refreshing showers of dew descend.'

Note

Apart from this description of Norfolk Island, Rev. Ullathorne's other mission in writing (according to historian Eris O'Brien, p. 61) 'was to persuade the labouring classes of England that their condition of life would not be improved, as they had imagined, by their deliberate entry into the convict ranks in Australia.' Transportation was not acting as a deterrent, but a means of escape from the misery of England and to the potential benefits once released. Ullathorne was a leading voice against the system of transportation. However, O'Brien asserts (pp. 66–67) that humanitarians such as Ullathorne were essentially 'short-sighted as they confined their efforts to reforming the morals of the poor, without tackling the political controls which brought about the social conditions and the crime.' Dickens probably would have shared the sentiment. (See Eris O'Brien, *The Foundation of Australia* *[1786-1800]* London: Sheed & Ward, 1937.)

10
An Illustrious British Exile
John Lang

George Barrington, pickpocket.[1]
Volume: 19 Number: 472 Pages: 454–56
Date: April 9, 1859
Fee: 3 pounds 3 shillings for 6 Columns.

A few years ago I made the acquaintance of an elderly lady, whose husband, so far back as 1799, held an official position, both civil and military, in the colony of New South Wales. Many anecdotes she told me of celebrated characters who had, in the words of one of them, 'left their country for their country's good.' With most, if not with all, of these celebrities the old lady had come in contact personally.

'One morning,' she began, 'I was sitting in my drawing-room with my two little children, who are now middle-aged men with large families, when a gentleman was announced. I gave the order for his admission; and on his entering the door of the apartment, I rose from my chair, and greeted him with a bow, which he returned in the most graceful and courtly manner imaginable. His dress was that of a man of fashion, and his bearing that of a

---

[1] George Barrington, whose real name was Waldron (1755–1804). Barrington was a famous Irish gentleman-thief transported to Australia in the early years of settlement. He arrived in Sydney in 1791 and was generally considered a reformed character, winning government positions (which included Chief Constable at Parramatta) and grants of land. He is reputed to have written several publications including, *A Voyage to Botany Bay* (1795) and its sequel published in 1802, although there is no evidence to this effect. He died in a lunatic asylum. See, *The Aust. Dict. of Biography*.

person who had moved in the highest circles of society. A vessel had arrived from England a few days previously with passengers, and I fancied that this gentleman was one of them. I asked him to be seated. He took a chair, opposite to me, and at once entered into conversation, making the first topic the extreme warmth of the day, and the second the healthful appearance of my charming children—as he was pleased to speak of them. Apart from a mother liking to hear her children praised, there was such a refinement in the stranger's manner, such a seeming sincerity in all he said, added to such a marvellous neatness of expression, that I could not help thinking he would form a very valuable acquisition to our list of acquaintances, provided he intended remaining in Sydney, instead of settling in the interior of the colony.

'I expressed my regret that the Major (my husband) was from home; but I mentioned that I expected him at one o'clock, at which hour we took luncheon; and I further expressed a hope that our visitor would remain and partake of the meal. With a very pretty smile (which I afterwards discovered had more meaning in it than I was at the time aware of), he feared he could not have the pleasure of partaking of the hospitalities of my table, but, with my permission, he would wait till the appointed hour,—which was then near at hand. Our conversation was resumed; and presently he asked my little ones to go to him. They obeyed at once, albeit they were rather shy children. This satisfied me that the stranger was a man of a kind and gentle disposition. He took the children, seated them on his knees, and began to tell them a fairy story (evidently of his own invention, and extemporised), to which they listened with profound attention. Indeed, I could not help being interested in the story, so fanciful were the ideas, and so poetical the language in which they were expressed.

'The story ended, the stranger replaced the children on the carpet, and approached the table on which stood, in a porcelain vase, a bouquet of flowers. These he admired, and began a discourse on floriculture. I listened with intense earnestness; so profound were all his observations. We were standing at the table for at least eight or ten minutes; my boys hanging on to the skirt of my dress, and every now and then compelling me to beg of them to be silent.

'One o'clock came, but not the Major. I received, however, a note from him, written in pencil on a slip of paper. He would be detained at Government House until half-past two.'

'Again I requested the fascinating stranger to partake of luncheon, which was now on table in the next room; and again, with the same winning smile he declined. As he was about, as I thought, to depart, I extended my hand: but, to my astonishment, he stepped back, made a low bow, and declined taking it.

'For a gentleman to have his hand refused when he extends it to another is embarrassing enough. But for a lady! Who can possibly describe what were my feelings? Had he been the heir to the British throne, visiting that penal settlement in disguise (and from the stranger's manners and conversation he might have been that illustrious personage), he could scarcely have, under the circumstances, treated me in such an extraordinary manner. I scarcely knew what to think. Observing, as the stranger must have done, the blood rush to my cheeks, and being cognisant, evidently, of what was passing through my mind, he spoke as follows:

' 'Madam, I am afraid you will never forgive me the liberty I have taken already. But the truth is, the passion suddenly stole over me, and I could not resist the temptation of satisfying myself that the skill which made me so conspicuous in the mother country still remained to me in this convict land.'

'I stared at him but did not speak.

' "Madam," he continued, "the penalty of sitting at table with you, or taking the hand you paid me the compliment to proffer me—yourself in ignorance of the fact I am about to disclose—would have been the forfeiture of my ticket-of-leave, a hundred lashes, and employment on the roads in irons. As it is, I dread the Major's wrath; but I cherish a hope that you will endeavour to appease it, if your advocacy be only a return for the brief amusement I afforded your beautiful children."

' "You are a convict?" I said, indignantly, my hand on the bell-rope.

' "Madam," he said, with an expression of countenance which moved me to pity, in spite of my indignation, "hear me for one moment."

' "A convicted felon, how dared you enter my drawing-room as a visitor?" I asked him, my anger again getting the better of all my other feelings.

' "The Major, madam," said the stranger, "requested me to be at his house at the hour when I presented myself: and he bade me wait if he were away from home when I called. The Major wishes to know who was the person who received from me a diamond necklace which belonged to the Marchioness of Dorrington, and came into my possession at a state ball some four or five years ago—a state ball at which I had the honour of being present. Now, madam, when the orderly who opened the front door informed me that the Major was not at home, but that you were, that indomitable impudence which so often carried me into the drawing-rooms of the aristocracy of our country, took possession of me; and, warmed as I was with generous wine—just sufficiently to give me courage—I determined to tread once more on a lady's carpet, and enter into conversation with her. That much I felt the Major would forgive me; and, therefore, I requested the orderly to announce a gentleman. Indeed, madam, I shall make the forgiveness of the liberties I have taken in this room the condition of my giving that information which shall restore to the Marchioness of Dorrington the gem of which I deprived her—a gem which is still unpledged, and in the possession of one who will restore it on an application, accompanied by a letter in my handwriting."

'Again I kept silence.

' "Madam!" he exclaimed, somewhat impassionedly, and rather proudly, "I am no other man than Barrington, the illustrious pickpocket; and this is the hand which in its day has gently plucked from ladies of rank and wealth, jewels which realised, in all, upwards of thirty-five thousand pounds, irrespective of those which were in my possession, under lock and key, when fortune turned her back upon me."

' "Barrington, the pickpocket!" Having heard so much of this man and of his exploits (although, of course, I had never seen him), I could not help regarding him with curiosity; so much so, that I could scarcely be angry with him any longer.

' "Madam," he continued, "I have told you that I longed to satisfy myself whether the skill which rendered me so illustrious in Europe still remained to me, in this country, after five years of desuetude?[2] I can conscientiously say that I am just as perfect in the art, that the touch is just as soft, and the nerve as steady as when I sat in the dress-circle at Drury Lane or Covent Garden."

' "I do not comprehend you, Mr. Barrington," I replied. (I could not help saying *Mister*.)

' "But you will, madam, in one moment. Where are your keys?"

'I felt my pocket, in which I fancied they were, and discovered that they were gone.

' "And your thimble and pencil-case, and your smelling-salts? They are here!" (He drew them from his coat-pocket.)

'My anger was again aroused. It was indeed, I thought, a frightful liberty for a convict to practice his skill upon me, and put his hand into the pocket of my dress. But, before I could request him to leave the room and the house, he spoke again; and, as soon as I heard his voice and looked in his face, I was mollified, and against my will, as it were, obliged to listen to him.

' "Ah, madam," he sighed, "such is the change that often comes over the affairs of men! There was a time when ladies boasted of having been robbed by Barrington. Many whom I had never robbed gave it out that I had done so; simply that they might be talked about. Alas! such is the weakness of poor human nature that some people care not by what means they associate their names with the name of any celebrity. I was in power then, not in bondage. 'Barrington has my diamond ear-rings!' once exclaimed the old Countess of Kettlebank, clasping her hands. Her ladyship's statement was not true. Her diamonds were paste, and she knew it, and I caused them to be returned to her. Had you not a pair of very small pearl-drops in your ears this morning, madam?"

'I placed my hands to my ears, and discovered that the drops were gone. Again my anger returned, and I said, "How dared you, sir, place your fingers on my face?"

' "Upon my sacred word and honour, madam," he replied, placing his hand over his left breast, and bowing, "I did nothing of the kind! The ear is the most sensitive part of the human body to the touch of another person.

---

[2] Desuetude: disuse.

Had I touched your ear my hope of having these drops in my waistcoat pocket would have been gone. It was the springs only that I touched, and the drops fell into the palm of my left hand." He placed the ear-rings on the table, and made me another very low bow.

'And when did you deprive me of them?' I asked him.

'When I was discoursing on floriculture, you had occasion several times to incline your head towards your charming children, and gently reprove them for interrupting me. It was on one of these occasions that the deed was quickly done. The dear children were the unconscious confederates in my crime—if crime you still consider it—since I have told you, and I spoke the truth, that it was not for the sake of gain, but simply to satisfy a passionate curiosity. It was as delicate and as difficult an operation as any I ever performed in the whole course of my professional career.'

'There was a peculiar quaintness of humour and of action thrown into this speech; I could not refrain from laughing. But, to my great satisfaction, the illustrious pickpocket did not join in the laugh. He regarded me with a look of extreme humility, and maintained a respectful silence, which was shortly broken by a loud knocking at the outer door. It was the Major, who, suddenly remembering his appointment with Barrington, had contrived to make his escape from Government House, in order to keep it. The Major seemed rather surprised to find Barrington in my drawing-room; but he was in such a hurry, and so anxious, that he said nothing on the subject.

'I withdrew to the passage, whence I could overhear all that took place.

' "Now, look here, Barrington," said my husband, impetuously, "I will have no more nonsense. As for a free pardon, or even a conditional pardon, at present, it is out of the question. In getting you a ticket-of-leave, I have done all that I possibly can; and, as I am a living man, I give you fair warning that if you do not keep faith with me, I will undo what I have already done. A free pardon! What? Let you loose upon the society of England again? The colonial secretary would scout the idea, and severely censure the governor for recommending such a thing. You know as well as I do, that if you returned to England to-morrow, and had an income of five thousand a-year, you would never be able to keep those fingers of yours quiet."

' "Well, I think you are right, Major," said the illustrious personage.

' "Then you will write that letter at once?"

' "I will. But on one condition."

' "Another condition?"

' "Yes."

' "Well, what is that condition? You have so many conditions that I begin to think the necklace will not be forthcoming after all. And, if it be not, by—"

' "Do not excite yourself to anger, Major. I give you my honour—"

' "Your honour! Nonsense! What I want is, the jewel restored to its owner."

' "And it shall be, on condition that you will not be offended, grievously offended, with me for what I have done this day."

' "What is that?"

' "Summon your good wife, and let her bear witness both for and against me."

'My husband opened the drawing-room door, and called out "Bessie!"

'As soon as I had made my appearance, Barrington stated the case—all that had transpired—with minute accuracy; nay, more, he acted the entire scene in such a way that it became a little comedy in itself; the characters being himself, myself, and the children, all of which characters he represented with such humour that my husband and myself were several times in fits of laughter. Barrington, however, did not even smile. He affected to regard the little drama (and this made it the more amusing) as a very serious business.

'This play over, my husband again put to Barrington the question: "Will you write that letter at once?"

' "Yes," he replied, "I will; for I see that I am forgiven the liberty I was tempted to take." And seating himself at the table, he wrote:

' "Mr. Barrington presents his compliments to Mr.—, and requests that a sealed packet, marked DN. No. 27, be immediately delivered to the bearer of this note. In the event of this request not being complied with, Mr. Barrington will have an opportunity ere long of explaining to Mr.—, in Sydney, New South Wales, that he (Mr.—) has been guilty of an act of egregious folly."

'Fourteen months passed away when, one morning, my husband received a letter from a gentleman in the colonial office. He clapped his hands, cried Bravo! and then read to me as follows:

' "My Dear Major,—The great pickpocket has been as good as his word. My lady is again in possession of her brilliants. Do whatever you can for Barrington in the colony; but keep a sharp eye upon him, lest he should come back and once more get hold of that necklace."

'My husband sent for Barrington to inform him of the result of his letter, and he took an opportunity of asking the illustrious man if there were any other valuables which he would like to restore to the original owners?

' "Thank you—no!" was the reply. "There are, it is true, sundry little articles in safe custody at home; but, as it is impossible to say what may be in the future, they had better for the present stand in my own name!" '

11
A Special Convict
John Lang

Sir Henry Browne Hayes—transported to NSW in 1802, who found a novel way of ridding his property of snakes.
Volume: 19 Number: 474 Pages: 489–91
Date: April 23, 1859
Fee: 2 pounds 12 shillings for 4 ½ Columns.

Sir Henry Hayes, said my informant (an old lady who had been the wife of a government official in New South Wales), was what was called in Sydney 'a Special.' Specials were gentlemen by birth and education, who had been convicted of offences which, however heinous in a legal point of view, did not involve any particular degree of baseness. For instance, Major B., who, in a violent fit of passion, stabbed his footman for accidentally spilling some soup and soiling the king's livery, which the Major was then wearing—was a Special: so was the old German Baron, of whom I may speak to you on another occasion: and so were those Irish gentlemen who took a prominent part in the rebellion, and escaped the fate that awaited Mr. Emmett— Specials. All these kind of criminals, up to the departure of General Macquarie, and the arrival of Sir Thomas Brisbane, were not treated like common thieves and receivers of stolen property, but with great consideration. If they were not emancipated immediately on their arrival, they were suffered to be at large, without the formality of a ticket of leave. They were, in short, treated rather as prisoners of war on their parole, than as prisoners of the Crown in a penal settlement. Grants of land were not given to them while they were in actual bondage, but they were permitted to locate themselves on any unoccupied pieces of land in the vicinity of Sydney. The greater number of them were well supplied with funds by their relations in England, Ireland, or Scotland, and erected very comfortable, if not particularly handsome, abodes, and laid out gardens and grounds. General Macquarie went a little too far, perhaps. He not only admitted them to his table, as soon as they were emancipated, but he elevated some of them to the magisterial bench.

Sir Henry built a pretty little cottage on the estate known as Vaucluse, and upon which the house of Mr. William Charles Wentworth now stands. There is not a lovelier site in the known world. Beautifully wooded with evergreens, the land covered with every description of heath, which is in bloom nearly all the year round; a lovely bay of semicircular shape, and forming one of the inlets of the magnificent harbour of Port Jackson spread out before the lawn, its dark blue waters laving the milk-white sand, some black rocks in the distance (known as 'the Bottle and Glass') standing out sufficiently far to cause the spray to beat continually over them, the north shore plainly visible across the broad expanse of water,—travel where you will the eye will not rest upon any spot more favoured by Nature than that exquisite valley which was called Vaucluse, in consequence of its resemblance in one or two respects to the Vallis Clausus where Petrarch, in the words of Lord Byron,

With his melodious tears gave himself to fame.

To put his crime out of the question, Sir Henry was a man of very great taste, and an Irish gentleman of the old school.

'What was his crime?' I asked, in my then ignorance of this colonial celebrity.

'He carried off by force and violence a young lady with whom he was passionately in love, and who had several times refused his offers of marriage. The penalty of the offence was transportation for life. I am not quite sure that he was not, in the first instance, sentenced to be hanged. My husband, in common with many officers, was partial to Hayes, who could be very witty and amusing, and who, whatever may have been his habits in early life, led a most temperate and exemplary life in the colony of New South Wales. He was surrounded by every comfort that money could purchase, and he was always glad to see persons of whom he was in the habit of speaking as 'those of my own order.' The only defect in his manner was, that his air was somewhat too patronising.

That Hayes was perfectly mad on the crime that led to his banishment, there could not be the slightest question; but upon all other points no one could be more rational. That his statements with reference to his case were untrue, no one who read the report of his trial could doubt for a single moment; but that Hayes himself believed his own version to be the correct one, was equally certain. I never saw Sir Henry but twice, and I must do him the justice to say, that on neither occasion, did he speak of his case. He was by far too well-bred to think of making the faintest allusion to it. By the way, he did once say in my presence, on the occasion of his killing a fly with the handle of a carving-fork, 'That's how I should like to crush John Philpot Curran'; but upon my husband remarking to him, 'My wife never heard of that person, Hayes'; Sir Henry made me a very low bow, begged me a million pardons, and instantly changed the theme.

'Why was he so inveterate with regard to Mr. Curran?' I inquired.

'It was Mr. Curran, my husband told me, who prosecuted Sir Henry Hayes', was the old lady's reply. I told you that I only saw Sir Henry twice, she continued. On the first occasion he called at our house, in a state of great nervous excitement. After being introduced to me, and speaking for a while on various subjects, he thus addressed my husband: 'My dear Major, for the last eleven days I have suffered agonies of mind, and have been praying, from early dawn to dusky night, almost without intermission, to my favourite saint, Saint Patrick. But he seems to take no more notice of me, nor of my prayers, than if I were some wretched thief in a road-gang, with manacles on my leg, and a stone-breaking hammer in my hand.'

'What is the matter, that you require the aid of Saint Patrick?' said my husband.

'The matter!' replied Sir Henry. 'You are aware, perhaps, that that part of the country where I live literally swarms with venomous serpents: there are black snakes, brown snakes, grey snakes, yellow snakes, diamond snakes, carpet snakes—in short, every species of snake in the known world. Now, so long as they confined themselves to the lawn and the garden, I did not so much mind. It was bad enough to have them there, but, with caution, I could avoid them. The brutes, however, have lately taken to invade the house. We have killed them in the verandah, and in every room, including the kitchen. Now, it was in consequence of this, that I addressed my prayers to Saint Patrick: and suggested that he might whisper to them to go into other people's houses, and not mine, in order to gratify their curiosity concerning the habits of civilised man: but to no purpose. Last night I found a gentleman, six feet long, and as black as a coal, coiled up in my white counterpane;[1] and another of the same dimensions underneath the bed. However, I am determined they shall not banish me from that abode, but that I will banish them; or, at all events, keep them at a proper distance—say a distance of at least fifty yards from any part of the house. And what I want you to do, my dear Major, is to render me some assistance in the matter.'

'What do you propose doing?' my husband inquired.

'You know perfectly well, my excellent friend,' continued Sir Henry, 'that Saint Patrick so managed matters that no snake could ever live on or near Irish soil. The very smell of it is more than enough for them. It will be a matter of time and of money; but to carry out my project I am most firmly resolved.'

'What do you propose doing? and how can I aid you?' said the Major.

'Hark ye!' returned Sir Henry. 'I intend to import to this country about five hundred tons of genuine Irish bog, which shall be dug from the estate of a friend of mine. It shall come out in large biscuit barrels. I shall then have a trench dug round my premises, six feet wide and two feet deep; and this trench the Irish earth shall fill.'

'And do you really believe that Australian snakes will be kept away by your Irish soil, Sir Henry?' said the Major.

'Believe? Of course, I do! I am quite certain of it,' responded Hayes. 'This very day I have written to my friend in Ireland, and told him to employ an agent to carry out my wishes, and have the bog-earth taken down to Cork for shipment. Now, the favour I have to ask of you is this: to write, in your official capacity, a letter to my agent, which I will enclose to him—such a letter as will lead the captains and doctors of the ships that touch at Cork to

---

[1] Counterpane: quilt, a bedspread.

fill up the complement of convicts for these shores, to suppose that the soil is for government, and required for botanical purposes; and further I want you to allow it to be consigned to yourself or the colonial secretary. Each ship might remove a quantity of its stone ballast and put the casks of bog in its stead. By these means I should get it all the quicker.'

'My husband endeavoured to laugh Sir Henry out of his idea; but in vain. He was firm, and said: 'If you won't assist me, I must instruct them to charter a ship for the especial purpose, and that would cost a very serious sum of money.'

My husband, of course, could not think of acting in the matter without previously obtaining the consent of the Governor, who was so amused at the superstitious character of Hayes' enterprise, that his Excellency caused the required letter to be written, and handed to him.

About a year afterwards, the first instalment of the soil arrived—some forty barrels—and was conveyed from Sydney to Vaucluse (a distance of six miles) by water; and within the next year the entire quantity had reached its destination. The trench, in the meantime had been dug, and all was now ready for 'circumventing,' as Sir Henry expressed it, 'the premises and the vipers at one blow.'

My husband and myself and a large party of ladies and gentlemen went down to Vaucluse in the government barges to witness the operation of filling in the trench. The superintendent of convicts—a country-man of Hayes' and who believed as implicitly as Hayes himself did in the virtue of Irish soil with regard to vipers—lent Sir Henry barrows and shovels and a gang consisting of seventy-five men—all of them Irishmen—in order to complete the work as rapidly as possible. Sir Henry, in person, superintended, and was alternately pathetic and jocular. Some of his running commentaries on Saint Patrick and his wonderful powers and some snatches of song that he sang in honour of the saint, convulsed with laughter all those who stood around him. The work over, one or two of the men asked for a small quantity of the sacred earth, and Sir Henry said: 'Well, take it and welcome; but I would rather have given you its weight in gold.'

Strange to say, from that time forward, Sir Henry Hayes was not visited by snakes. They did not vacate the grounds in the vicinity of Vaucluse, but none were ever seen within the magic circle formed of the Irish earth. Whether the charm is worn out and whether the Wentworth's are invaded as was Sir Henry, I know not. But this I know, that Captain Piper, who held the appointment of naval officer in the colony, to whom Vaucluse was subsequently granted, and from whom Mr. Wentworth purchased it, assured me that during the many years he lived there with his family, no venomous reptile had ever been killed or observed within Hayes's enclosures, notwithstanding they were plentiful enough beyond it.

I wish the reader to understand that I have simply related the above story as it was told to me, and that I do not offer any opinion as to the efficacy or otherwise of Irish soil in keeping away Australian snakes from any spot upon which it may be placed.

After a pause, the old lady resumed:

I ought to have mentioned that it was on the seventeenth of March, Saint Patrick's Day, that this curious ceremony was performed, and that at its conclusion, at half-past four in the afternoon, we dined with Sir Henry in a large tent formed of the old sails of a ship, which were lent to him for the occasion by the captain of the vessel then lying in the harbour. Sir Henry was in excellent spirits, and when the evening closed in, he sang several Irish melodies with great sweetness and pathos. To every one present he made himself extremely agreeable, and, on the whole, I never spent a happier day in my life, albeit I was the guest of a Special convict.

12
Baron Wald
John Lang

A story of a transported convict (a German Baron) which includes descriptions of the environs of Liverpool, a district outside Sydney; and also Norfolk Island.
Volume: 19 Number: 476 Pages: 537–41
Date: May 7, 1859
Fee: 3 pounds 13 shillings and 6 pence for 7 Columns.

What led to the old gentleman's misfortune, said the old lady, who told me the story of Sir Henry Hayes,[1] that is to say, what crime he had committed, I am not quite sure; but I think my husband said the Baron's offence was following to England a countryman of his own, and shooting him in the streets of London, in order to avenge the wrong which the victim had inflicted on a member of his ancient family. As the offence was committed on British soil, he became amenable to British laws, which punish murder with death, except in those cases where the sovereign exercises his prerogative—as George the Third did in the case of the Baron, who, immediately on his arrival, was provided with separate apartments in the prisoners' barracks, and informed that he might employ his time as he pleased. There could be no question that the Baron was a person of some importance in Germany; for I happen to know that special instructions were forwarded from home to the Colonial Government, and periodical reports required as to his state of health and the nature of his occupations. It was, in short, evident that,

---

[1] [Original footnote] See 'A Special Convict.' [*Household Words*, 23 April 1859, No. 474, pp. 489–91; see also p. 104 in this volume].

although the old Baron had grossly violated our laws, and had paid, or was paying, the modified penalty thereof, he was still regarded by some of the loftiest in the mother country, as an object of sympathy and commiseration.

My husband had a grant of land about seventeen or eighteen miles from Sydney. Through this land the river—called George's River—runs. There are several very pretty sites for houses; but there is one in particular, where the river bends itself very fantastically, and tall Australian oak-trees grow upon the very edge of the banks. The river is not very broad, not broader, perhaps, than the Thames at Eton.

It was not my husband's intention to build on this property. He merely wanted it as a place where he might keep a few brood mares; and a few cows—just sufficient to supply us every week with butter. The land was fenced in, and a hut erected thereon; but nothing further was laid out upon this grant of three hundred and twenty acres, to which no name even had yet been given. It was usually alluded to as the George's River farm. You must know that in those days, officers connected with the administration of affairs had farms in all directions. Many were grants, many were purchases. Land was of very little value then. This very place of which I am speaking, was not worth more than sixty pounds. No one would have given fifty pounds for it. Why, four acres and a half in George Street, nearly opposite to the barrack gates, my husband sold to a man who had been a regimental tailor, for the following articles:

> Twelve dozens of port wine.
> Six gallons of Hollands.[2]
> Two pieces of broadcloth.
> Twenty-five pounds of American tobacco.
> One chest of tea.
> Two bags of sugar.
> One set of harness for gig.
> One saddle and bridle.
> One single-barrelled fowling-piece.

---

[2] Hollands: gin made in Holland.

Two canisters of powder, and
Four bags of shot.

And a noble bargain it was considered by every one: though I have lived to see that same allotment sold in little pieces, and realise upwards of fifty thousand pounds. Where the Post-Office now stands was the boundary of our paddock. But never mind these stupid statistics, which have really nothing to do with the old Baron.

One day the Major was driving out in his gig to visit this George's River farm, and give some instructions to the servant in charge of it, when he overtook the Baron, about four miles from Sydney walking along the Parramatta Road. The Major pulled-up, and inquired the destination of the old gentleman.

'I am going,' said he, 'to George's River to see Colonel Johnstone, from whom I wish to ask a favour. I called at Annandale, and they told me that the Colonel had ridden to the farm, and I am now in pursuit of him.'

The Baron had made himself a perfect master of the English language, though he spoke with a foreign accent.

'Jump in, Baron,' said the Major; 'I, too, am going to George's River.'

They had not driven far before they overtook the Colonel. He was talking to an elderly man in the Road—a man whom my husband recognised as one who had been a sergeant in the regiment when Colonel Johnstone marched it to Government House, deposed Governor Bligh, and placed himself at the head of affairs.

'Did you know Colonel Johnstone?' I asked.

My husband, replied the old lady, was a captain in the regiment; but, fortunately for him, he was not at the head of his company when it proceeded to enforce that strong measure. Colonel Johnstone was the godfather of my eldest boy. I can remember his giving an account of what took place on that memorable occasion of his deposing Governor Bligh. 'We could not find him for a long time,' said he, 'and at last discovered him under a bed. We had to pull him out by the legs, for he would not come out of his own accord, nor when I commanded him.' The Colonel was sentenced by the court martial that was held upon him in England, to be shot. But his interest was too powerful to admit of the sentence being carried out, and he was suffered to return to and end his days in the colony.

My husband, who knew the Colonel's temperament so well, saw that he was in anything but a good humour; and, whispering to the Baron to forego his request for the present, they bade the Colonel 'Good day!' and drove on at a rapid pace.

'The favour that I wished to ask Colonel Johnstone is this,' said the Baron, 'to permit me to occupy a small piece of land on this farm of his; and in return I will take care that his fences shall not be destroyed, and his cattle stray away. I do not like the locality of Sydney. I care not for ocean scenery. I wish to be in a lonely place, and live on the banks of a pretty river.'

'I have just such a place on this farm of mine which we are approaching,' said the Major; 'and if you approve of it, we shall have no difficulty in agreeing about the terms, Baron.'

A few minutes afterwards the Major and the Baron were standing on the site I have already described to you. The latter was in ecstasies; and, clasping his hands, exclaimed, 'Wie herrlich! wie friedlich!' (How charming! how peaceful!)

The terms were very soon settled. The Baron was to rent that piece of land in the centre of the grant, containing in all about ten acres, and henceforward to be known as Waldsthal, on a lease for twenty-one years, at one dollar per year, paid quarterly. Spanish dollars and cents were the currency in those days.

There was an abundance of timber of all kinds, and available for building purposes, on the land; and the Major could at all times, command as much convict labour as he pleased, including artisans of every class. He drafted from the barracks, sawyers, carpenters, blacksmiths, plasterers, labourers, and subsequently painters and glaziers. These men were sent to the farm, and placed at the disposal of the Baron. They were previously informed that any disobedience or disrespect towards the Baron, would be visited by summary corporal punishment at Liverpool (then a little out-settlement three miles from the farm), and a transfer to an iron-gang. Insomuch as the Major, though far from being a cruel man or a hard master, invariably kept his word with the felonry of the colony, there was not the least occasion for him to repeat the admonition; and at the end of three months there was erected on Waldsthal one of the prettiest little weather-boarded cottages that the imagination can conceive. The Baron was his own architect, and had combined comfort with good taste. There was his little dining-room, about thirteen feet by twelve; his little drawing-room, of the same dimensions; his little library; his store-room; and his cellar, and larder; and his hall. The bedroom and dressing-room were the only large rooms in the cottage. The flower and kitchen gardens were also very prettily laid out, and proportioned exactly in size to that of the cottage. On the whole, it was a perfect gem of a cottage residence; and it was furnished with neatness and a simplicity which were really touching.

Now and then—say half a dozen times in the year—the Major and myself used to visit the Baron, and spend the day with him. Upon all occasions, while walking round the grounds with him, the old gentleman was to me very communicative. Amongst other things, he told me that he had never been married; but that he had a sister who was the mother of three sons and two daughters; that he had served in the army of his native country, and that the military decorations which were suspended over his fire-place in the drawing-room were the rewards for his services in various fields of battle. These little matters, together with his sword, he said, had been forwarded to him through the kindness and consideration of a distinguished military man of rank in the service of the King of England.

Generally, we gave the Baron notice of our intention to visit him; but on several occasions, when we had suddenly made up our minds for the excursion, we omitted this little formality, and took our chance of finding him ready to receive us. It would not have been strange had a gentleman living, like the Baron, in almost utter seclusion in the Bush, been negligent of his personal appearance. But it was not so. Go when we would—with notice or without notice—we found him invariably as cleanly in person, and as neat in his attire, as though he had been a resident of any capital in Europe, and in the habit of daily mixing in its society. One Saturday afternoon, when we invaded him unexpectedly, we found him in the farmyard, superintending the feeding of his poultry; but dressed, as usual, à la Frederick the Great, in Hessian boots, a brown velvet coat, elaborate frills and ruffles, a pigtail, and a three-cornered hat. His establishment consisted of two men servants (convicts assigned to the Major) and an old woman who had been transported, but emancipated shortly after her arrival in the colony, for giving timely notice of an intended rise and general revolt amongst the convicts in Sydney and its vicinity. This old woman did the washing and the cooking, and kept the cottage in that very good order on which the Baron, doubtless, insisted. He was not a witty man by any means; but he had an unexhaustible stock of entertaining anecdotes, which he told remarkably well, and at the proper moment. He was, moreover, an excellent musician, and played upon the violin with the skill of a professor. Moreover, he took likenesses with a facility and faithfulness which were truly astonishing.

A few years after he had first taken up his abode in the cottage, the Baron was presented with a free pardon which bore the autograph of his Majesty George the Third; and he was informed that if he desired to return to Germany, the Colonial Government were instructed to provide him a passage in any vessel in which he might think proper to select a cabin. It was painful to witness, as I did, the emotion of the old Baron, when the Major communicated to him this piece of information. The King's pardon he was compelled to accept, and he did so in the most graceful manner; but he expressed a wish to remain at his 'little paradise' on the George's River farm, so long as he lived, and on his death that he might be buried there.

In all, the Baron lived at Waldsthal for eleven years; and, during that period, had several visits from those pests called Bushrangers. On the first occasion they handcuffed the Baron and the old woman together, and locked them up in the stables, whence they were unable to effect an escape. The men servants they tied separately to trees, and bound them so tightly they could not extricate themselves. For upwards of forty hours they did not taste food or drink. When discovered by the merest accident, they were all nearly famished. The culprits were captured several months afterwards and were hanged in the jail at Sydney for a series of robberies on the highway. (The old Baron, by the bye, declined to give evidence against them.) The Major asked for the dead bodies, and they were given up to him. He caused them to be suspended in chains, from the bough of a large tree on the Liverpool Road, and nearly opposite, though half a mile distant from the old Baron's cottage.

This, however, did not operate as an example or terror to the desperate criminals with whom we had to deal, for the next party, four in number, who went to rob the Baron, cut down the dead bodies; and, locking the Baron and his household up in the same room with them, rifled the premises and took their departure. These men were also captured and hanged. At the Baron's request the Major did not ask for their bodies. He (the Baron) said they were very disagreeable people to come in contact with, when living; but if possible, worse, when they had been dead some time.

The Major's turn came for doing duty at Norfolk Island as commandant, and we went to that terrestrial paradise, where the clinking of chains and the fall of the lash rang in the ear from daylight till dark—these sounds accompanied occasionally by the report of a discharged musket and the shriek of some wretch who had fallen mortally wounded. These shots became so frequent that, at last, they ceased to disturb us, even at our meals. Our house was behind a rampart, surmounted by a battery of guns, loaded to the muzzles with bullets, bits of iron, tenpenny-nails,[3] and tenter-hooks.[4] By day and night sentries guarded the doors with loaded muskets and fixed bayonets. 'Kill the Commandant!' was always the first article of the agreement these desperate monsters came to when they entertained an idea of escape. In the morning when they were brought out, heavily ironed, to go to work, the guard that had been on duty all night was drawn up opposite to them. The relieving guard then came from the barracks; and, in the presence of the Commandant, obeyed the order Prime and load. Then came the ringing of the iron ramrod in the barrel. Then the order Fix bayonets; followed by the flashing of the bright steel in the sun's rays. Many a time have I, from my window, seen these incorrigibles smile and grin during this ceremony, albeit they knew that, upon very slight provocation, they would receive the bullet or taste the steel.

During the twelve months that we were on the island one hundred and nine were shot by the sentries in self-defence, and sixty-three bayoneted to

---

[3] Tenpenny-nails: nails sold at ten pence a hundred.
[4] Tenter-hooks: a frame or endless track with hooks used for stretching and drying cloth.

death, while the average number of lashes administered every day was six hundred. Yet, to my certain knowledge, almost every officer who acted as commandant at Norfolk Island tried to be as lenient as possible, but soon discovered that, instead of making matters better, they made them worse, and they were in consequence, compelled to resort, for security's sake, to the ready use of the bullet and bayonet, and the constant use of the lash. That part of the punishment which galled these wretched prisoners most was the perpetual silence that was insisted upon. They were not allowed to speak a word to each other. One day when the Major was inspecting them, they addressed him through a spokesman, who had been originally a surgeon, and who had been transported for a most diabolical offence. He was a very plausible man and made a most ingenious speech, which he finished thus:

'Double, if you will, the weight of our irons and our arm-chains, increase the weight of the logs attached to our legs, reduce the scanty amount of the food we now receive by way of ration; but, in the name of humanity, permit us the use of our tongues and our ears, that we may have, at least, the consolation of confessing to each other the justice of the punishment we have to undergo!'

The Major turned a deaf ear to this harangue, and, when he related it to me, laughed at it. I, however, very foolishly took a very different view of the case, and teased him into trying the effect of such indulgence. What was the result? The use they made of their tongues was to concoct a plan for butchering the garrison and every free man, and seizing the next vessel that brought a fresh cargo of convicts to the island. The moment the expected vessel was signalised was to be the moment for the general rise and the desperate attack. There would have been a frightful encounter and awful bloodshed, and it is impossible to say which side would have gained the mastery. It was a Jew who betrayed his fellow criminals, and gave my husband the information just in time; for on the morning following the expected vessel hove in sight. The convicts, however, were all safely locked up, and had their bread and water handed in to them through the strong iron bars of the small windows of their cells. My husband called a council of war, and it was resolved that several of the ringleaders should be shot. For doing this, by the way, he received a severe reprimand from the Governor of New

South Wales, who informed him that it was his duty to send them to Sydney to be tried and hanged. This, next to effecting an escape, would have been precisely what the culprits most desired. The Jew who gave the information was sent to Sydney (his life would have been taken on the island), a ticket-of-leave was granted to him, and he became a street hawker. Subsequently, he was emancipated, and became an innkeeper and money-lender. Eventually he obtained a free pardon, visited England, bought a ship and cargo, and became a merchant. He is now in possession of landed and other property of enormous worth. The first time I saw that man he was a manacled felon, working on Norfolk Island amongst his compeers in infamy. The last time I saw him he was lolling in a handsome carriage, dressed in what he conceived the acmé of fashion, and was drawn by two thoroughbred horses. So that, so far as he was concerned, the words which my husband's predecessor caused to be cut upon a piece of stone, and placed over the gate of the prison-yard, were not applicable—Lasciate ogni speranza voi ch'entrate.[5]

In talking of Norfolk Island I have lost sight of the dear old Baron. While we were away, we received a letter from him in which he stated he had been visited for a third time by Bushrangers, but that they had not robbed him, they had only been guilty of a mauvaise plaisanterie.[6] They had merely made him and the old woman exchange garments, and dance for them while they drank some spirits and water and smoked their short clay pipes. It was very humiliating to him, he remarked, but to them it was, no doubt, very funny.

Eventually the old Baron became very ill. Several military surgeons went to see him; but they all declared to my husband that his case was a hopeless one. And so is proved to be; for he lingered on till he died. Amongst his papers was found a will—a very short one—by which he bequeathed to my husband (whom he appointed his sole executor) all that he might die possessed of in the colony of New South Wales. His effects, as may be supposed, were not very valuable intrinsically; but we prized them very

---

[5] *Lasciate ogni speranza, voi ch'entrate* (Italian): 'Abandon hope ye who enter here' [from Dante's *Divine Comedy*].
[6] *Mauvaise plaisanterie* (French): a rude or ill-mannered jest.

highly in remembrance of the old gentleman. He was buried at Waldsthal, and his tombstone is still there. The cottage was accidentally burnt down, and the place has since become a ruin.

13
Three Celebrities
John Lang

The stories of three transported convicts.
Volume: 19 Number: 477 Pages: 553–57
Date: May 14, 1859
Fee: 5 pounds for 9 ¾ Columns.

Fox, Pitt, and Burke were (said the old lady)[1] low London thieves, who were transported under the names of the three most celebrated orators and statesmen of their time. Their offence was picking pockets at a fair, and their sentences fourteen years. Charles James Fox was assigned to my husband, and we employed him in chopping wood, cleaning the knives, brushing clothes, and carrying messages in the absence of the orderly. He was a slight young man of about twenty-four years of age, and far from ill-looking, when he first came into our service. For a few months he conducted himself remarkably well, but subsequently he became idle, negligent, and addicted to speaking the most flagrant untruths: so much so, that the Major on several occasions had him flogged. On the last occasion he never returned to us. He watched his opportunity, and made his escape from the constable who had him in charge. He was, of course, gazetted as a run-away, and a reward of ten pounds offered for his apprehension. A few days afterwards the gazette contained the names of William Pitt and Edmund Burke. They, too (most probably at the instigation of Charles James Fox), had run away from their

---

[1] [Original footnote] See our last number, p. 537. ['Baron Wald', *Household Words*, 7 May 1859, No. 476, pp. 537–41; see also p. 110 in this volume].

respective masters. It was rather droll to see those three great names placarded in all directions, and the persons who then bore them in the colony minutely described. Pitt's master was a Doctor Wylde whom we knew very intimately. He described Pitt to us as a short, thick-set, and rather determined character. Edmund Burke, having been originally a compositor, was employed in the government printing-office, which was then superintended by Mr. George Howe, who was afterwards permitted to publish a newspaper in Sydney, subject to the censorship of the Colonial Secretary. Burke, according to Mr. Howe's account, was a man of good natural ability, but of violent and, when excited, ferocious disposition.

The career of these men who took to the bush (considering that it extended over a period of eight years), was a very remarkable one. There was not a road in the colony, not even a cross-road or bush-road, upon which they had not stopped and robbed travellers. And it is a mistake to suppose that the police was an inefficient body in those days. It was more efficient than they are very likely to be again. Some of the police had been highwaymen, poachers, gamekeepers,—men who had been pardoned for capturing bushrangers guilty of great crimes, and who had received their appointments in consequence of the proofs they had given that confidence might be placed in them. Their pay was small, and the rewards for the apprehension of desperate characters were large. The pay of the great George Lewis, the most renowned of all Australian thief-takers and bushrangers, was only four dollars (one pound currency) per week, and, as he kept two horses, and maize was commonly two dollars a bushel, you may readily imagine that he had to look to the walls, and not to his pay, for a livelihood.

'What do you mean by looking to the walls, my dear madam?' I said.

All runaway convicts and bushrangers, she replied, were placarded on the walls and gate-posts, as well as advertised in the government gazette. I have seen the walls of the police-office in Sydney literally covered with these hand-bills, headed £10. Reward! £25 Reward! £50. Reward! £100. Reward! The great thief-takers, men of George Lewis's stamp, and they were all men of prowess, courage, and sagacity—never hunted in couples. They always went forth alone. They were not only too greedy for the gain, but too jealous of each other, to admit of their combining, to effect the capture. They depended upon strategy and individual valour, rather than upon numbers, to accomplish the ends they had in view. It was a curious sight to see a group of these thief-takers (blood-hounds they were called) coolly spelling a fresh placard on the walls of the police-office, and then observe the speculation which was stamped upon their various countenances. My husband of course knew all these men, and so did I for that matter; and when Charles James Fox became such a very distinguished man in his way, all of them, not in a body, but separately, came to make certain inquiries touching his habits and peculiarities.˘

The Major was [away] from home when Mr. George Lewis called, and I received him in the breakfast parlour, and answered all the questions he put to me, 'Did Charles James Fox drink? Could he read and write? Was he a talkative or a silent sort of a man?' I answered that Charles James Fox did *not* drink; he could *not* read or write, and that he *was* a silent sort of a person. 'Burke can read.' said Mr. Lewis, 'but he is not much of a hand at writing; and as for Billy Pitt he doesn't know a pothook from a hanger.' He then went on to say that he had had great hopes of taking, or bringing in dead, two out of the three lately, but that such hopes had been blighted: that he had hired a horse and cart and had gone up the Parramatta Road dressed as a farmer, in an old white top coat, leather leggings, and a round hat; that on the first occasion, he went and returned unmolested; but that, on the second occasion, he was stopped by two men armed with fowling-pieces, near the Iron Cove Creek, Ashfield; that they demanded his money or his life; that he said they should have it; that dropping the reins, and putting his hands into the hind pockets of the old top-coat, he discharged, through the pockets, a brace of loaded pistols, within a yard of each man's breast, and brought them both down as dead as hammers; that what with the five pounds ten shillings ready money that he paid for the top-coat, the hire of the horse and cart at one pound a-day, the bother and trouble of bringing the corpses to Sydney, and the loss of time, the job did not pay him, for they had only been at large three weeks, and the reward for them was a paltry ten pounds a-head; that he felt quite sure at the time that they were two of the three he was angling after; and that he never felt so disgusted in the whole course of his life as when he had them looked at, at Hyde Park Barracks, and found out his mistake. Mr. Lewis spoke so very feelingly on the subject, that, horrible as was the theme, I could not help pitying him, albeit I was constrained to smile—especially when he remarked quietly and seriously, 'It was a thousand pities that I shot them, mum; for in six or seven months from this time they would have been really worth having.'

One beautiful afternoon, in the month of October, I was on my way to the factory at Parramatta to select a female (convict) servant. I had a friend, a Mrs. Stellman, with me in the phaeton; and on the box was a groom as well as the coachman. My friend and myself were chatting away very cosily, and were approaching Homebush—an estate some ten or twelve miles from Sydney—when three voices called out 'Stop!' and presently from the thick brushwood that skirted the road, there emerged three men, one of whom I immediately recognised as our late servant, Charles James Fox, who, at the same moment, recognised my features. The three men were all armed, and Pitt and Burke had their fowling-pieces levelled at the men on the box. At first, Fox was startled, and I fancied I saw the man blush; but, speedily recovering himself, he hoped I was quite well, and that the Major and the children also had their health. Had I been alone I should certainly have read Mr. Fox a lecture, and have advised him to throw down his gun, and to give himself up to me. But as Mrs. Stellman was a good deal alarmed, I deemed it prudent to get away from the trio, as quickly as possible. Touching his straw hat, in the most respectful manner imaginable, Mr. Fox said, 'I didn't know this turn-out, mum. It is new since I left, or I should never have thought of stopping you, mum. Be so good, mum, as to assure the Major that he has nothing to fear from me and my companions here.' This speech was very pleasing to my ears; and, with a slight inclination of my head towards Mr. Fox, I ordered the coachman to proceed. Fox had then been a bushranger for upwards of twelve months.˜

As soon as I arrived at Parramatta, I reported to Mr. Kherwin, the chief constable, all that had taken place, and he at once took horse, accompanied by several of his myrmidons,[2] and went in pursuit of Fox, Pitt, and Burke.

---

[2] Myrmidons: a subordinate or follower who carries out orders without scruple or hesitation.

But, to no purpose. They had such secure hiding-places in the various localities they frequented, that they baffled every effort to discover them. And they were so cunning in their movements, that even the Aborigines—the blacks—could not track them down. These strangely-gifted people—so far as sight is concerned—discovered several of their dens; but the birds had always flown. After a while, by the way, the blacks declined to track bushrangers; and, if pressed to do so, would put the police on a wrong scent. The tribes in the vicinity of Sydney, Parramatta, and the other infant towns, had been intimidated, and several of their numbers shot by those lawless men.

As you appeared to take some interest in my friend, Mr. Barrington, I may mention that I met that illustrious personage on that afternoon at the factory in Parramatta, where he then held the situation of under-superintendent of convicts. He seemed very much amused when I recounted my adventure on the road, and observed, with his wonted humour and quaintness: 'Well, madam, it was an act of gallantry and of generosity—considering how often the Major had caused him to be flogged—which could scarcely have been expected at the hands of a plebeian thief—a contemptible London pickpocket.' Mr. Barrington did not even smile when he said this; but assumed an air of extreme seriousness—emphasising the words plebeian and contemptible with marvellous dexterity, so as to convey to me that he did not, at that moment, intend to allude to the eminent and aristocratic position which he had formerly held in his profession. Unintentionally, I wounded his feelings; or else his look was a consummate piece of acting, when, in answer to the question I out to him, 'Why do you not consult your ingenuity, and capture these three men?' he replied: 'Ah. madam, in my leisure hours I pursue literature not bushrangers. I am, at this present time, writing a play—a comedy in five acts—and founded on an incident in my own life.'

I could not help saying, 'I beg your pardon, Mr. Barrington,' and then expressed a hope that I should have an opportunity of seeing his piece performed.

'It is for the London boards,' he replied; 'but I shall be proud to submit it to your judgment, previously to transmitting it to the committee at Drury Lane.'

'Did he keep his promise?' I inquired.

'Yes,' said the old lady, 'and a clever play it was. In some scenes it was very pathetic, in others comical in the extreme. There was not, however, a single coarse word in it, nor an allusion that could offend the most fastidious prude in Christendom. The title of the piece was, *All The World's A Swindle.*'

'And the plot?'

'Of that I have only an indistinct recollection, but the story is something of this kind. On the Doncaster race-course, the great pickpocket, a Mr. Shenstone meets a nobleman in the betting-ring, and loses to him a hundred guineas, which he pays in gold. Mr. Shenstone's manners and his equipage that of a man of a gentleman, and his equipage that of a man of fashion and of fortune. The nobleman is charmed with Mr. Shenstone and the next day, when he meets him on the course he greets him with a polite bow, which is returned by one equally polite. They speak; they make another bet, for another hundred guineas; Mr. Shenstone loses, and with very great good humour pays his money to the nobleman, partly in gold and partly in bank notes. That evening he calls at the hotel where the nobleman is staying, with his wife and daughter, a very handsome girl of eighteen years of age, and represents that a man from whom he had won a bet—a farmer-looking person, but evidently a sharper—had paid him in forged bank-notes, and as he had parted with some of these notes before he was aware of the fraud that had been committed, he was anxious to discover into whose possession they had come, in order that he might receive them back, and give good notes or gold in return.˝

The nobleman and Mr. Shenstone carefully examine the notes which the former received; but amongst them no forgeries are found; they are all genuine. This examination lasts for some time, and, during its continuance, the lady and her daughter enter the sitting-room. Mr. Shenstone rises from his chair, and is thereupon introduced to the ladies, who become as much fascinated by the polished manners and discourse of the stranger as my lord is himself. Mr. Shenstone is invited to stay tea, which is about to be served.

He accepts. And thus (what the great pickpocket desires) an acquaintance is established—an acquaintance which is renewed in London, some weeks afterwards, at the theatre, much to the great pickpocket's advantage, for he contrives to despoil his friend's friends of jewels worth five times the amount he lost on the race-course. When informed of this he observes, with great truth. 'That thief Barrington! Who else?' My lord gambles very deeply, falls into serious difficulties, secretly purloins his wife's diamond bracelets, has a paste set made to resemble them, and sells the real brilliants to a jeweller, who disposes of them to an old duchess, from whose person the great pickpocket steals them, and at once proceeds to the box of the lady, who is sitting decked out in her paste. He informs her that Barrington is in the house, and advises her to place her jewels in her pocket. She does so. He then abstracts the paste gems, places the real diamonds in their stead, revisits the old duchess, who, intent on the play, has not yet discovered her loss, and around her aged wrists clasps the mockeries! Partly love for the young girl, and partly respect for her mother, forms the motive for this action.'

'Was the piece ever played?'

'The captain of the vessel to whom Barrington had entrusted it, lost it on the voyage to England. But let me continue with my story of Fox, Pitt, and Burke. I was on another occasion, doomed to see their faces. The Major and myself were returning from the farm at George's River. We had been on a visit to old Baron Wald, and had driven out in the gig. It was a beautiful moonlight night, and when we neared a place called the Iron-Bark Forest, some thirteen miles from Sydney, we were commanded to Stop! by three men, two of whom presented their fowling-pieces at us, whilst the third said:

' "Now, then, what have you got?"

' "Is that you, sir?" said my husband, who recognised the man's voice, for it was Fox who spoke.

' "God bless me, Major!" was the response. "I beg you many pardons."

' "Rob him!" cried out one of the others. "If he had been my master, and had flogged me, I'd shoot him!"

' "No! no!" said Fox. "It was agreed that old masters were to go free, and when we wanted to rob old Howe, the other day, being very badly off for money, you reminded me of our agreement, and I now wish you to be reminded of it." '

The Major parleyed with them for at least a quarter of an hour, and reproved them for shooting a constable a few weeks back. They replied that the constable had insisted on capturing them, and that they had acted only in self-defence. Their capture, eventually, was curiously effected.

During the fifth year they had been at large they suddenly disappeared from the roads. They had not been seen, or heard of, for so long that it was imagined they had either made their escape from the colony, by some extraordinary means, or that they had, like some other bushrangers whose remains were found, been lost in the bush, and perished of hunger. Such, however, was not the case. They had penetrated the interior to a distance of fifty miles from Sydney, and had located themselves at a place not very far distant from a lofty mountain called Razorback, in consequence of its peculiar shape. Here they established themselves, built a log-house, enclosed several acres of land. which they cropped, and made a rather extensive garden for the growth of vegetables. They also built stock-yards and outbuildings for the cattle and the horses of which they possessed themselves. The luxuries of convict life—such as tea, sugar, tobacco, spirits, et cetera—they had, previous to their retirement from business, stored up in very large quantities. They had, moreover, taken with them to their farm three convict women, whom they had (nothing loth) carried away from the services, respectively, of the persons to whom they paid marauding visits.

They had taken away with them, from the house of a settler whom they plundered, a large black Newfoundland dog. Three years and seven months after the dog was stolen, he, one morning, to the astonishment of his master, returned, jumped about, and barked in an ecstasy of delight. The master of the dog (a Mr. Sutter) was afraid that the bushrangers, Fox, Pitt, and Burke, were about to pay him a second visit; and, summoning his servants, and arming them, he laid in wait and in ambush for their approach, determined to take them under any circumstances, dead or alive. But the bushrangers came not. From an examination of the dog's neck, it was quite evident that he had been kept continually on the chain, and that he must have broken his collar, and made his escape. Mr. Sutter, who lived within five or six miles of

Parramatta, on the branch road to Liverpool, mounted his horse, and had an interview with Mr. Kherwin, the chief constable.

There could be no question that the dog had broken loose, and found his old master; but, then, by what road had he come back? There was then no regular road beyond Liverpool. Those who had settled further in the interior had only their own push tracks as they were called. If the dog they thought could be put upon this track by his master no doubt he could be coaxed to show the way to the abode of the bushrangers. It suddenly occurred to Mr. Kherwin that the blacks, having no idea of the end in view, would have no scruples in pointing out the direction whence the dog had come and tracking him for five or six miles. This was determined upon; and taking with him a strong force, well armed, Mr. Kherwin returned with Mr. Sutter to his farm, and early on the following morning the expedition set out. The blacks were not long in finding the foot-prints of the dog, at some distance from the house, and began to run down the track at the rate of three or four miles an hour. Mr. Sutter and the dog accompanied the expedition. At noon there was a halt for refreshment, and then the pursuit was continued till evening when the camp was formed, fires lighted, and the arms piled in readiness for any attack—not that there was any danger of such a thing in that lonely and untravelled region of the new world.˜

The dog, strange to say, appeared to be very sulky, and showed no disposition to render the slightest assistance. On the following afternoon the blacks came upon the imprint of a man's boot. They now began to suspect the truth, but they had gone too far. It was now a matter of compulsion, and not of choice. Towards evening one of the blacks from a considerable eminence pointed to some smoke which was issuing from a valley in the distance—a valley which was completely shut in on three sides by small mountains, and bounded on the fourth side by a clear and broad stream of water. An enchanting nook, as Mr. Kherwin described it to me. After proceeding a few hundred yards in the direction of the smoke, the barking of dogs was audible and the lowing of cattle; and ere long, a house and outbuildings became visible. Mr. Kherwin and Mr. Sutter then deliberated as to whether they should descend and commence the attack at once; or whether they should defer the operation until after nightfall, when they would most probably have retired to rest; or whether the attack should be delayed until the following morning just before daybreak. It was resolved, eventually, that while the daylight remained they should creep down to the edge of the valley, and there conceal themselves until ten or eleven o'clock. when they would march upon the abode, surround it, and call to the inmates to come out and surrender.

This resolution was acted upon; but the bushrangers' dogs had kept up such a loud and incessant barking during the advance of the invaders, that the trio had arisen from their beds, lighted a candle, armed themselves, and come outside the door. Fox, Pitt, and Burke could be seen by the light of the candle in the house; but they could not see their enemy; for the night was dark. Nothing could have been easier than for Mr. Kherwin and his party to have fired a volley and shot them as they stood; but the chief constable could not make up his mind to this; nor would Mr. Sutter have seconded such a proposal. At length Mr. Kherwin, when within only twenty yards of them, called out, in a very loud voice, 'We are twelve in number: lay down your arms this instant, or you are dead men. Our pieces are levelled at you.' They threw down their arms, retired within the house, and barred the door. Fortunately for Mr. Kherwin's party they had no lanthorn or candle with them; for, had they shown a light, some of the party would have fallen to a certainty. What was now to be done?

The besiegers approached the door of the house and desired the bushrangers to come out; but they returned no answer. To break in upon them was impossible, for there were no crowbars, pickaxes, or other such weapons at hand; while the numerous dogs on the premises became so vehement and desperate, it was necessary to shoot and bayonet several of them. Matters remained thus until the morning, when the besiegers withdrew to a distance of about sixty yards from the house, and there took up a position in a stock-yard. The besieged, however, opened fire from loopholes, and in less than a quarter of a minute twelve rounds of ball-cartridges were discharged from as many firelocks. Fortunately none of the shots took effect. It was therefore deemed prudent to withdraw, for the present, to a distance of one hundred yards, and stand behind a clump of large gum-trees. Nevertheless, the besieged, whenever they saw a head, or a hand, or a foot, had a shot at it. From the number of shots with which they were simultaneously greeted, Mr. Kherwin believed that there were at least nine bush-rangers in the house: and, as he was unprepared for an encounter of this character—each of his party having only twenty rounds of ammunition—he was compelled to reserve his fire. The house, thickly-coated as it was with mud, was bullet-proof. Mr. Sutter, therefore, at Mr. Kherwin's instigation, rode into Parramatta for reinforcements, taking with him several of the blacks as guides. The Commandant at Parramatta, sent a sergeant and ten private soldiers to Mr. Kherwin's aid.

It was not until the third day, however, that they arrived at the scene of action; for they had to take with them two light field-pieces, six-pounders, and a variety of implements for effecting an entrance in case the mud-casing to the house should resist the cannon-shot for any length of time. The news soon arrived in Sydney, and numbers of officers and gentlemen, many of whom had been robbed on the road by Fox, Pitt, and Burke, hastened to the spot.

On the morning of the second day, after the arrival of the military, one of the shots from a field-piece happened to strike the door of the stronghold, and shiver it to atoms; whereupon a woman, with her hair streaming down her back, and holding in her hand a large white rag at the end of a stick, came out of the house, and, approaching the besiegers, cried out, 'We surrender!' The firing ceased, and the woman was permitted to return and communicate to the bush-rangers that only ten minutes would be allowed them to come out, unarmed, and give themselves up. This they did, and were forth with ironed and handcuffed.

The women, it seemed, had aided them in firing at the authorities. Fox, Pitt, and Burke, having trained them to the use of fire arms, and made them expert marks-women. In the house were found no less than thirty fowling-pieces, twelve pairs of pistols, powder and shot in large quantities, lead for casting bullets, and several swords and cutlasses. The abode itself had been cleanly kept. Everything was in the neatest order; while the land, considering that the bush-rangers were but amateur agriculturists, was very well tilled. In the dairy was found both butter and cheese of their own making; in the store-house salted beef and pickled pork of their own curing. In short, there were very few farms in the colony better stocked. They had abundance of poultry and pigeons.

Fox, Pitt, and Burke were all hanged in the Parramatta jail. The women pleaded that they had been taken away by force; and, as the plea was accepted they were placed in the factory. These women were all under sentence of transportation for life; but a few years afterwards they obtained tickets of leave, became the wives of expirées, and led tolerably respectable lives.

Several officers made application to the governor to have the bushrangers' farm granted to them, and one of them had the good fortune to obtain it.

14
Kate Crawford
John Lang

The story of a convict woman, the daughter of a Yorkshire squire, who made a fortune in Australia.
Volume: 19 Number: 478 Pages: 596–600
Date: May 21, 1859
Fee: 4 pounds 14 shillings and 6 pence for 9 Columns.

'We had several female Specials,' said the old lady;[1] 'but the most remarkable of them was Kate Crawford, or beautiful Kitty, as she used to be called. She was very handsome, certainly, and not more than nineteen when she arrived in the colony.'

'What had been her condition in life?' I asked.

'She was the daughter of a Yorkshire squire. In short, she was a lady by birth,' was the reply, 'and had received the education of persons in her father's position and circumstances, and she was accomplished, according to the standard of that day.'

'And what was her crime?'

'Horse-stealing!'

'Horse-stealing?'

'Yes. That was the offence of which she was convicted, and, in those barbaric days, sentenced to be hanged. That sentence, however, was commuted to transportation for fourteen years.'

---

[1] [Original Footnote] See page 553 of the last Number. ['Three Celebrities' *Household Words*, 14 May 1859, No. 477, pp. 553–57; see also p. 120 in this volume].

'Rather a strange offence for a young lady to commit,' I remarked.

'Very true; but you must hear the particulars, just as she related them to me and to several other ladies who took a very great interest in her. And remember that all she told us—I mean all the facts she stated—corresponded exactly with those detailed in the report of her trial, which was subsequently, at her request, obtained from England. In one sense of the word, Kate was a very bold girl; in another sense, she was the very reverse of bold. Her manners were in perfect harmony with her person—soft, gentle, and feminine; but, if she were resolved upon carrying out any project, great indeed must have been the obstacle she would not surmount. Her story, as she told it, was this:

'My father, Squire Crawford and one Squire Pack lived within a mile of each other. Their estates adjoined. Squire Pack had a son, John Pack, of about twenty-four years of age. I was then between seventeen and eighteen. John Pack was an only son, and I was an only daughter. Both Squire Pack and my father were widowers, and had housekeepers. The old people, over their bowls of Punch one night, settled that John Pack should be my husband. Now, it so happened that John Pack—whom I liked very much, he was such a good-natured goosey—was already in love, and secretly engaged to a farmer's daughter, a stout, tall, red-haired girl, with blue eyes, and a very florid, but clear, complexion. Just the girl, in short, to captivate poor John, whose taste was not particularly refined. She had, besides, the exact amount of learning to suit poor John, who was not an erudite person by any means. I, too, had a secret engagement with a younger son of Sir Francis Bowman, and who was a lieutenant in a regiment of foot. Squire Pack and my father were both great tyrants, and to have offered the slightest opposition to their plans would possibly have led to their putting into execution, respectively, that threat which was constantly on the lips of either of them: I'll turn you out of doors; and cut you off with a shilling! John Pack and I therefore came to an understanding.˜

We were to be lovers in the presence of the old people; but to every other intent and purpose, we were to assist each other in corresponding with our true loves—trusting as we did, to some accident or some quarrel between our fathers to annul the marriage contract they had entered into on our behalf.

Matters went on this way for several months, and nothing could be more satisfactory to us young people. John Pack frequently carried letters and messages for me, and I as frequently did the same for him. Squire Pack and my father used to quarrel once in every year, and for a month or two were the most implacable enemies: but, at the end of such term, the one or the other would give way, make an advance (which was always met), shake hands, and become as good friends as ever. The truth was, that when the evenings drew in, they missed their game of cribbage; for John Pack was a very sleepy person over cards, and, as for myself, I could never play at any game except beggar-my-neighbour.[2]

'One morning in the month of December the hounds met a few miles from our house. Squire Pack and my father rode to cover together. John Pack, who had brought me a letter from my lover, accompanied them and joined the meet. The moment they were out of the gate I broke the seal and read as follows:

' "Dearest Kate,—If you possibly can, meet me on the Halifax road, near The Hen and Chickens. I will be there at eleven, an I will wait till two in the hope of seeing you. I have something very important to communicate, *My* father intends having an interview with *your* father, the day after to-morrow. I would have ridden over to the Hatch, only you gave me such good reasons for not doing so, or even coming *near* the place at present. In haste.

'Ever affectionately yours,

' "George Bowman."

'The Hen and Chickens, a roadside inn, was distant from the Hatch (the name of my father's house) about six miles; and when I received my lover's letter it was nearly half-past ten o'clock. I flew to the stables, and ordered the groom to saddle my horse. To my disgust, he informed me that the animal was as lame as a cat. I then ordered him to put my saddle on Marlborough, a second hunter of my father's. The groom told me that the horse had been taken to a point called Milebush, where the Squire expected to pick him up fresh. I then said "Saddle the old mare," and was given to understand that she had gone to the farrier's to be shod. What was to be done? I deliberated for a

---

[2] Beggar-my-neighbour: a card game for two players.

few minutes, and then ordered the groom to take my side-saddle and bridle and follow me to Squire Pack's, and hastily attiring myself in my riding-habit and hat, I ran across the fields as fast as I could, and made for the stables of our neighbour. The only saddle-horse in the Squire's stables at the time was a magnificent thorough-bred colt, which had just been broken in; and this colt the Squire's groom was not disposed to saddle for me without the Squire's personal order. Becoming very impatient, for it then wanted only three minutes to eleven, I shook my whip at the groom, and said: "Saddle him this instant! Refuse at your peril! You shall be discharged this very night!" All Squire Pack's servants as well as our own believed that I was to be John Pack's wife, and the groom, fearful of that gentleman's wrath, no longer hesitated to obey my instructions. The colt was saddled and brought out. I mounted him, and laid him along the road at the very top of his speed, perfectly satisfied that John Pack would take care that my father never heard of my adventure, and that his father would say nothing about it—determined as I was to have a note for John, to be delivered on his return from the chase.

'It was exactly nineteen minutes past eleven when I arrived at the Hen and Chickens, and found George Bowman waiting for me. He had walked over from his father's house. The colt I had ridden was so bathed in perspiration that I alighted, and caused him to be taken into a shed and rubbed down. While the stable-boys were so engaged, George and I walked along the road, and discoursed intently on our affairs for more than an hour and a-half. We then returned to the inn, and I gave orders for the colt to be saddled. But, alas! the colt was not in the stable wherein he had been placed after he had been rubbed down, nor was a traveller, who was dressed like a gentleman, and who had come to the inn to bait his jaded horse, shortly after my arrival, to be found on the premises, though his horse was in one of the stalls—a horse that must have been a very swift and valuable creature in his day, but then rather old and broken-winded. There could be no doubt that this person, whoever he might be, had made the exchange, and ridden away unseen while the stable-boys were taking their dinner. A well-dressed man had ridden swiftly past George and myself whilst we were walking on the road; but we were far too much engrossed in conversation to take any particular notice of himself or the steed he was riding. Under these awkward and distressing circumstances, I scarcely knew what to do.˜

'It was now past two o'clock, and I was anxious to return to my home. I, therefore (accompanied by George Bowman to the very edge of our grounds), proceeded on foot. As soon as I was in my own room I divested myself of my riding-habit, and wrote a letter to John Pack, requesting him to see me at the earliest moment possible. It was past four o'clock when my father returned, and the moment I saw him I discovered that he was much the worse for the refreshment he had taken while absent from home. He told me, and it was quite true, that John Pack had had a bad fall in the field, had broken his thigh and smashed his head, and that he was then lying in a dangerous state at a public-house not far from Bradford. I begged of him to let me go and see the sufferer. But he said No! and then informed me that he had had such a violent quarrel with Squire Pack, that they could never be on speaking terms again. It was all about the settlements, he said; that the old thief wanted to hold off coming down with any money till his death; that he (Squire Pack) had broken his word; that he (my father had given him a good bellyful of his mind; that he told the Squire that neither he, nor his father before him, were born in wedlock; and that, after all, it would be a disgrace for a Crawford to have a Pack for a husband.˜

'All this distressed me very much; but I still hoped that this, like their other quarrels, would be made up ere long, and that, in the meantime, poor John Pack would recover, and Sir Francis Bowman tempt my father to listen to the liberal proposals he was about to make to him with respect to my union with George. It was, however, a frightfully anxious night that which I passed. My sleep, when it at last stole over me, was a troubled one, and my dreams a succession of horror upon horror. When I awoke, I fancied that all was a dream—the accident to John Pack, the quarrel between my father and the Squire, the meeting between myself and George Bowman, and the loss of the colt at the Hen and Chickens. But, alas! I was speedily awakened to the reality, by my father calling out "Kate! Kate! Come here! What have you been about? Here are the officers of justice come to take you before the Magistrate!" I ran down-stairs, confessed everything, and entreated him to forgive me. Like most of the old squires, he was a very violent and headstrong man, and on this occasion his anger was terrific. "Take her!" he cried to the officers. "Take her away! Let her be hanged, for all I care! She deserves it for deceiving me?"

'It seems that as soon as Squire Pack heard of my taking the colt away, he vowed that he would have me tried for horse-stealing, and thus would he disgrace the man who had called him such vile names and said such bitter things to him. And, in fulfilment of this vow, he went to the nearest magistrate, accompanied by his groom and another servant, and made a deposition upon oath. The magistrate was an old clergyman, to whom Squire Pack had given the "living," and who was in the habit of responding the words "of course," to every sentence the Squire uttered. A warrant for my apprehension was immediately issued, and I was taken into custody. What happened before the clerical magistrate I cannot recollect; but I can remember being asked several times, "What has become of the colt?" and replying, "I don't know." The consequence was, I was committed to take my trial at the forthcoming assizes, and was meanwhile sent to prison.

'Whilst I was in those cold and dismal cells, my father never came near me; nor did he write to me, or even send me a message. The only person whom I saw—and that was in the presence of the jailor—was George Bowman, who did all in his power to console me, although, poor boy, his face and shrunken form plainly betrayed that he was bordering on insanity, caused by grief. George told me that Sir Francis Bowman had spoken to Squire Pack: but the Squire would not listen to him, and that he had declined to receive the value, or double the value, of the colt which had been "stolen" by me—swearing, that "the law should take its course."

'The day of trial came, and I was arraigned. George Bowman had retained an able lawyer to defend me, but his advocacy was of no avail. He urged that I had not taken the colt with the intention of stealing it, but of returning it, after I had ridden it. To this the other counsel replied, "Why didn't she return it?" "Because it was stolen from her at the inn," was the rejoinder. This the jury regarded as a very fond (foolish) tale, and found me guilty; whereupon the judge put on the black cap, and sentenced me to be hanged by the neck until I was dead!

'What happened afterwards—whom I saw or what they said—I know not. I was in a perfect lethargy, and did not recover my senses until more than half of the voyage to the colony was completed.'

Here the old lady paused for a brief while, and then resumed.

'What Kate's sufferings must have been, when she was conscious of what was passing around her, it would, indeed, he difficult to describe. She had not only to bear the companionship of the three hundred degraded wretches who were her fellow-passengers; but to withstand the unseemly attentions of the Navy surgeon, who had charge of the convicts, and who had become enamoured of her extreme beauty. The captain of the vessel, also, fell desperately in love with her, and on several occasions proposed to marry her, abandon the sea, and settle in the colony. The surgeon having heard of this, quarrelled with the captain, and threatened Kate that if she ever spoke or listened to the captain again, he would have her hair cut off, and that she should be publicly flogged. (He had the power, you know, of inflicting such punishment upon any female convict who incurred his displeasure.) The captain being informed by one of his officers of this threat, thrashed the surgeon on the quarter-deck, to the delight of the women who looked on and cried "Bravo!" The surgeon called the guard—fifty soldiers (recruits). But as each man had his sweet-heart on board, and as the cause was regarded as the "woman's cause," the guard declined to interfere in the matter. This was a sad state of affairs, no doubt so far as discipline was concerned; but it tended very materially to Kate Crawford's advantage. Amidst the strife and contending passions of the two men, she was safe in that sense of the word most desirable to herself. When the ship arrived in the harbour, the surgeon preferred a complaint against the captain and his officers. There was an investigation which resulted in a manner rather prejudicial to the surgeon, and the Governor gave an order that he was not to be permitted to depart the colony until the pleasure of his Majesty's Government was known. Such pleasure was known about a year afterwards. It was to the effect that the surgeon was to be sent to England, under an arrest, in the first man-of-war[3] that touched at Port Jackson. He had made several statements and

---

[3] Man-of-war: warship.

admissions at the investigation, to warrant and insure his dismissal from the service of the state.

'Soon after her arrival, Kate had to undergo fresh persecutions. She was "applied for" by at least twenty unmarried officers, each of whom was anxious to have her "assigned" to him as a servant. It was not uncommon in those days for officers to marry their assigned servants, and make them sell rum at the back doors of their private houses, or quarters, to private soldiers and convicts at a dump (fifteen pence) a glass. It was by these means that many of them amassed their large wealth in ready money.'

'Did the Government know of this?' I asked.

'That is a question I decline to answer,' replied the old lady. 'But this I know, that when the duty was taken off rum imported to the colony, very few people were licensed to keep public houses. However, none of these gentlemen were destined to be the master of Kate Crawford. The statement she made at the investigation aroused the sympathy of Mrs. Macquarie (the Governor's wife), who enlisted the respect and affection of all who knew her. Mrs. Macquarie was driven in her private carriage to the Factory at Parramatta—an institution to which all unassigned convicts were taken on their arrival in Sydney—and had an interview with the unfortunate girl. I accompanied Mrs. Macquarie on that occasion.

'When Kate was brought by the matron superintendent into the little room in which Mrs. Macquarie and myself were seated, she was dressed in the uniform garb of females under sentence of transportation; the commonest calico print gown, a white apron, white cap without frills or strings, thickly soled shoes, and no stockings. The dresses were made short, so that the ankles and the lower part of the legs were visible, while the arms were perfectly bare from the elbow joint. Nevertheless, in those hideous garments, Kate still preserved the bearing of a well-bred gentlewoman. There was no low curtsey—no "May it please your ladyship"—no folding of the hands; but there was a gentle inclination of the head and of the body, and an honest, modest look, which would at once have satisfied the most suspicious person in the world that the girl was incapable of committing any crime. And when Mrs. Macquarie, with a graceful movement of the hand, requested her to be seated, she thanked, and obliged the old lady, simultaneously.

' "I have not come to see you out of mere curiosity," said Mrs. Macquarie, "nor have I come to gloat over the sight of a young lady in such a position as that in which you are now placed. I simply come, armed with the authority of the Governor, to know by what means your sojourn in this colony may be rendered the least painful."

'On hearing these words of unexpected kindness, the poor girl burst into passionate tears, and Mrs. Macquarie and myself followed her example.

'When she was calmed, and in a condition to listen, Mrs. Macquarie again put the question to her, and the poor girl replied, in broken accents: "Do with me, or for me, whatever your kind heart may dictate."

' "Then you shall live," said Mrs. Macquarie, "in private apartments, in the house of Mr. Kherwin, the chief constable of Parramatta, whose wife shall make you as comfortable as circumstances will admit of. Under that roof you will be perfectly safe, and protected from every species of annoyance. And if you will allow me, I will send you the means of providing yourself with more suitable apparel than that you are now wearing."

'Poor Kate expressed her gratitude in becoming terms, and we took our departure. Mrs. Macquarie then ordered the coachman to drive to the house of the chief constable, and expressed to that functionary her wishes, which were tantamount to orders; and that very night Kate Crawford occupied a room in the small but cleanly cottage of the Kherwins. They were very respectable people, the Kherwins; and Mrs. Macquarie arranged that Kate was to board with them. I don't know whether Kherwin and his wife were recompensed by a payment of money, or a grant of land, but I am quite satisfied that they lost nothing by the attentions they showed to their unhappy charge.

'Whenever the Major and myself went to Parramatta, we never failed to pay Kate a visit, and have a long chat with her. On one occasion she told us that she had received a reply to a letter she had written to a friend in England. Her old lover, George Bowman, she said, had, shortly after her conviction, become insane, and was a hopeless lunatic in an asylum. Her father had married a young damsel, and had by her an infant son. John Pack, when he recovered, and came to know of the cruel course of conduct his father had pursued, quarrelled with the old man, flogged him in his passion, and then married Peggy, and became a farmer on his own account. Squire Pack, too, had married a young maiden, and had made up his quarrel with Squire Crawford.

'Kate was only three years a prisoner of the Crown, or (to speak in the coarser phrase) a convict. General Macquarie, one morning, accompanied by Mrs. Macquarie, all the chief officials, and their wives, journeyed from Sydney to Parramatta. The cortège drew up opposite to the chief constable's cottage. The General and Mrs. Macquarie were the only persons who alighted. After a brief absence they returned, bringing with them poor Kate Crawford, whom the General handed into his carriage, and then ordered the postilion[4] to go to Government House. (There is a Government House in Parramatta.) There, in the presence of all assembled, the dear old General presented Kate with the King's pardon, and at the same time handed to her a piece of parchment, sealed with the seal of the colony, and bearing the General's own signature. It was the title-deed of a grant of land, of two thousand acres, within forty miles of Sydney, and situated in one of the best and most alluvial districts. This ceremony over, the old General led her to the dining-room, where luncheon was ready. The poor girl—she was then only twenty-three—was evidently much overcome by her feelings; but she struggled hard to subdue them, and succeeded.'

'And what became of her?' I asked.

'You shall hear,' said the old lady. 'While she was under the protection of the chief constable, Kate was not idle. She assisted Mrs. Kherwin in all matters connected with the household. The cows, the pigs, the poultry, &c., had each and all some share of her attention. And she kept the accounts—for the Kherwins sold the product of the animals which they reared. In short, although she did not cease to be what the vulgar call "a fine lady," she made herself a woman of business, and a shrewd one too,—not that she ever took an advantage of those with whom she dealt.

'Now free to do what she pleased, and with a grant of land in her possession, Kate resolved upon remaining in the colony, and devoting herself to farming and the rearing of cattle. Both the General and Mrs. Macquarie

---

[4] Postilion: a courier or swift messenger.

were so fond of her, that any favour she asked was at once accorded. She applied for fifteen convicts; they were assigned to her. She then engaged a very respectable overseer—a man of firmness and integrity. She borrowed three hundred pounds, where-with to commence operations, and build a house. At the end of two years she paid off this debt and had a considerable balance in hand. The wheat and the Indian maize grown upon her farm always brought the highest prices in the market, and she was equally fortunate with her live stock. Many offers of marriage were made to her, year after year, by persons in eligible positions and circumstances; but Mrs. Crawford, as she now called herself, had determined on remaining single. She had built for herself a vehicle called a sulky, a gig which had a seat for the accommodation of one person only, and in this she used to drive to Sydney once in every year. Upon all these occasions she was a guest at Government House. In eighteen hundred and twenty-three, she was the owner of twelve thousand pounds in money, which was invested on mortgage of landed property in the town of Sydney; and in eighteen hundred and thirty-seven, when I last saw her, and laughingly said, "You must be frightfully rich by this time, Kitty," she replied, "Well, if I were to die now, there would be about one hundred and twenty thousand pounds to be divided amongst those who are mentioned in my will. Your boys are down for a few pounds—not that I fancy they will ever want them."

'Is she still alive?' I asked.

'Yes,' replied the old lady, 'and likely to live for the next twenty years; for although she had many days of sorrow, she never had one of sickness, to my knowledge.'

[Since the history of Mrs. Crawford was related to me, she has departed this life. The gentleman who gave me this information lived many years in Australia. On asking him what she died possessed of, he answered: 'The value of her estate, real and personal, was as nearly as possible half a million Sterling.']

15
Miss Saint Felix[1]
John Lang

A young gentlewoman transported to Sydney for murder.
Volume: 19 Number: 479 Pages: 613–17
Date: May 28, 1859
Fee: 4 pounds 4 shillings for 8 Columns.

She was not handsome; but she was very very pretty—the prettiest little Irish girl that I ever beheld! said the old lady.[2] She had golden hair and dark blue eyes, a compact and elastic figure, and the tiniest feet and hands. She was not more than eighteen when she landed in Sydney as a convict, under sentence of transportation for life. She did not arrive till eighteen hundred and twenty-seven or eighteen hundred and twenty-eight; and during the administration of Sir Ralph Darling. The Special System was now utterly defunct, and all convicts were to be treated alike, without the least reference to what had been their former condition.

In point of strictness there was no doubt, very proper and very just; but to those who remembered the lenient administration of General Macquarie and Sir Thomas Brisbane, it appeared harsh in the extreme.

---

[1] Saint Felix: names and titles were extremely important to Dickens and articles had to follow his style. The name Felix, (Latin for happy or happiness) is likely to have been a very deliberate choice.

[2] [Original footnote] See page 596 of the last volume. ['Kate Crawford', *Household Words*, 21 May 1859, No. 478, Vol. 19, pp. 596–600; see also p. 132 in this volume].

The Major and myself left Sydney shortly after the departure of General Macquarie from the colony, and went to live on an estate, which had been granted to us, in the vicinity of Campbell Town. The Major sold his commission, and had now nothing further to do with public life. He was still in the Commission of the Peace; but that was all.

The girl, Annie Saint Felix, whom I have mentioned, was assigned to some neighbours of ours (our nearest neighbours, for they lived only six miles off), the Prestons', and very nice people they were. Captain Preston early in life had held a commission in the Foot Guards, and inherited a considerable fortune; but having run through his money, he sold his commission and retired, with the proceeds, to the wilds of Australia, and became a settler. Mrs. Preston, who was a lady of aristocratic birth and breeding, was one of the kindest-hearted beings in existence, and their son's and daughters, a goodly number of each, ranging from fourteen to three years of age, were without any exception, remarkably fine and well-behaved children. The eldest was a daughter.

One morning I had a visit from Mrs. Preston. She wanted to ask my advice, she said, on a very delicate matter, that she scarcely liked to act upon her own judgment, and Captain Preston had declared himself incompetent to assist her. On asking her what was her difficulty, the following dialogue took place between us:

'You are aware,' she began, 'that I applied for a needlewoman?'

'Yes,' I replied. 'Have you got one?'

'No; but a young girl has been assigned to us who can do needlework.'

'Then, that is all you require of her?'

'True. But she happens to be a young lady by birth, and is, moreover, a highly educated girl.'

'Well, she is none the worse for those qualities, as you only want her for needle-work. What was her crime? Did you ask her?'

'Yes, and she replied, 'Murder, madam! My brother was hanged; but I am sorry to say they spared my life!' '

'Murder? Dear me. Did you question her further?'

'No,' said Mrs. Preston. 'When she pronounced the word murder, my blood ran cold, and I trembled from head to foot. Now, what I wish to ask you is, would you keep a girl under your roof who had been guilty of such a crime?'

'What sort of a disposition has she?'

'She is as gentle, seemingly, as she is pretty and graceful. It was, indeed, her kind and gentle manner towards the children, and her well-selected language that induced me to say to her, on the third day she had been with us—yesterday, in fact—when we were alone in the nursery, 'Dear me, Annie, what could have brought a girl of your stamp and education to this colony ?' Of course, as soon as she pronounced the word murder, I lost all power of speech, and have scarcely spoken to her since. To tell you the truth I feel rather afraid of her.'

'Pretty girls have often a wicked expression of countenance. Has she one?'

'On the contrary, she has a voice like that of a bird. I wish you would come over, see her, talk to her, and tell me what you think of her. You can stay the night, you know.'

Mrs. Preston had aroused my curiosity. When I was one of the lady visiting matrons of the factory at Parramatta,[3] I had discoursed with several women who had committed murder in England, Ireland, or Scotland; but they were all women of a very inferior station in life. I agreed to accompany my friend, and as soon as the Major had completed his (unpaid) magisterial duties on the bench, and had returned home, we all three set out together;

---

[3] Female Factory at Parramatta: an overcrowded and squalid establishment where women were put to work, originally weaving coarse cloth (in 1819 it moved to a bigger purpose-built building). The women were sorted in three classes: general, merit and crime. In 1823 a treadmill was installed essentially for the crime class of prisoner to work upon. It was also a place convict women could find sanctuary from domestic abuse or go to when pregnant or ill. There were eventually nine Female Factories in three colonies (NSW, Tasmania and Qld). They also served as arrival depots for women and the main place where female labour could be acquired by settlers, and men could go to find wives. Robert Hughes described them as an 'equivalent to an Australian version of a mail-order-bride establishment.' See, Hughes, *The Fatal Shore: a History of the Transportation of Convicts to Australia 1787–1868*, pp. 255–58.

Mrs. Preston driving me in her gig, and the Major riding, on the right-hand side, on horseback.

When I first saw the girl I was very much struck with her appearance. Her hair was brushed back off her forehead, and arranged as plainly as possible. On her head was a little white three-cornered cap, such as all maid-servants wore in those days; her dress was of common drugget[4] of a dark chocolate colour, and around her slender waist was tied a gingham apron, which Mrs. Preston had given to her. She was then sewing and talking to the little children, who were playing around her knees. When we left the nursery, I exclaimed to Mrs. Preston:

'That a murderess! I do not believe her.'

'But,' urged Mrs. Preston, 'she says she is; and why should she confess to having committed so diabolical a crime, if it be untrue?'

Figure 1.6 Female penitentiary or factory, Parramatta by Augustus Earle, c.1826. Image courtesy of National Library of Australia: nla.pic-an2818460.

---

[4] Drugget: coarse woollen or part-woollen material used for clothing.

While Captain Preston and the Major were drinking their claret after dinner, and were talking about their crops and their cattle, Mrs. Preston and myself paid another visit to the nursery. By the light of the wood fire and the candle, the girl looked even prettier than by daylight. After Mrs. Preston had put several questions to her, concerning the children and the work she had in hand, and had received the girl's replies, I said:

'Your mistress has told me that which I can scarcely credit. She tells me you were convicted of murder.'

'It is quite true, madam,' said the girl, blushing almost crimson.

'What could have prompted a girl like you,' I said, 'to think, even, of taking the life of a fellow-creature?'

'I will tell you, madam,' she sighed.

'Sit down, Annie; you must be tired after your day's labours,' said Mrs. Preston, taking a chair near the fire (an example which I followed).

The girl obeyed—sat down opposite to us, and, gazing steadfastly at the blazing logs on the hearth, in the following words told her story:

'My brother (who was five years my senior) and myself were orphans, and were living under the roof of an uncle (my father's eldest brother), on an island in the north of Ireland. We had a cousin, one of the loveliest and most amiable girls that ever lived, and she was engaged to be married to a Mr. Kennedy, a gentleman of large property, who lived on the same island, and within a few miles of my uncle's house. When all was prepared for the wedding, this gentleman—if he deserves the title of gentleman—broke off the match. That was cruel enough, seeing that our cousin loved him devotedly; but he had the wickedness to express, as a reason for his baseness, a suspicion which, if true, would have blasted not only my cousin's character, but that also of my brother. The horrible nature of this accusation, and its utter falsity, added to her disappointment, so preyed upon the girl's mind, that, after pining in hopeless grief for a month, she sunk into her grave: dying of a broken heart. On the night of her burial, my brother, frantic with rage and grief, vowed that, on the first opportunity that presented itself, he would take Mr. Kennedy's life. I knelt beside him, and vowed that I would share in his revenge.

For weeks and months Mr. Kennedy, who knew the determined character of my brother, and of the vow that he had made, kept within the boundaries of his own estate. This, however, did not calm our passionate feelings. On the contrary, it exasperated them, and our purpose had become the more settled. Often and often would my brother say to me, and I to him, 'Are you steadfast in your vow?' And the answer we invariably gave each other was 'Yes.' One afternoon—about four months after the death of our cousin—one of the servants informed my brother that Mr. Kennedy had been seen riding in the direction of a little fishing town. He immediately ordered his own horse and mine to be saddled; and, arming himself with a brace of pistols, we both galloped in pursuit of Mr. Kennedy. We had not ridden more than three miles when we saw him. As we galloped on the turf, and not on the hard road, he did not hear the sound of our horses' hoofs until we were close upon him. As soon as he recognised us, he put spurs to his horse; but his steed was not so swift of foot as were ours, and, just as he was entering the town, we overtook him. He then became deadly pale, and begged for mercy. But in vain. I seized his horse's bridle, and said, 'Now, Francis,' whereupon my brother put his pistol to Mr. Kennedy's left breast, and drew the trigger. Mr. Kennedy fell from his horse—a dead man! Such was the crime for which my brother lost his life on the scaffold, and for which I was sent to this colony for the term of my natural life. I wished to die with my brother; but it was willed otherwise.'

'And do you not repent?' I asked.

'Yes,' the girl sighed. 'I try to think of my cousin's sufferings, and of her death, and of the pain, the agony of mind, which my uncle and every member of our family endured, when Mr. Kennedy falsely branded us with dishonour; but the deep dye of my crime weakens even those recollections, and my life is a life of remorse and mental expiation.' Here she paused; and, hiding her face with her hands, she shed tears.

At this moment Mrs. Preston's eldest son, a boy of twelve years of age, came into the nursery, and said, 'Papa wants some more wine, mamma. Will you send him the keys of the cellarette?'[5] On observing the girl shedding

---

[5] Cellarette: a cabinet for bottles of wine, liquor, glasses etc.

tears, he approached her; and, placing his hand gently on her shoulder, he said, in a very gentle tone of voice which touched both his mother and myself:

'What is the matter, Annie? I hope mamma has not been scolding you?'

'No, Master Charles,' she replied. 'Your mamma has been very kind to me.'

'Then why do you cry?' the boy demanded.

Mrs. Preston and myself rejoined our husbands, leaving Master Charles with the girl, to whom, in common with all his brothers and sisters, he was already very much attached. Even before we left the room, he patted her upon the head, and begged her to dry her eyes.

Captain Preston and the Major were both much moved, when we recounted to them what we had just heard. Had it been previous to eighteen hundred and twenty, which was about the date of General Macquarie's departure from Sydney, we should have had very little difficulty in doing for Annie Saint Felix what had been done for Kate Crawford; or, at all events, we could have obtained for her a conditional pardon, which would have rendered her a free woman in the colony and its dependencies. But, with the then governor, so far from having any interest, the Major and Captain Preston were such objects of dislike, that they were never invited to the government-house. This was in consequence of the opinions they had openly expressed of the governor's conduct, in having two private soldiers flogged in the barrack-square, and drummed out of the regiment, after they had been sentenced to be transported by the Civil Tribunal. The fact was that the men died of the severe flogging they had received—the one in the jail, and the other in the general hospital, to which institution he was removed in his last moments. The names of these men were Sadds and Thompson.

So far as my husband was concerned, an order was secretly passed that no more convict-servants were to be assigned to him; but to Captain Preston this order had not yet been extended, inasmuch as he had been less emphatic in his denunciations. Into the merits of this question I have no wish to enter. No doubt too much leniency had been shown during the two preceding administrations; but I am, nevertheless, disposed to think that Sir Ralph Darling rushed into the opposite extreme, and by the adoption of so severe a code led to those dissensions between the governed and the governing, which convulsed the colony till the arrival of his successor, Sir Richard Bourke.

'But what became of Annie Saint Felix?' I asked.

She remained with the Prestons for five years. She was to them a perfect treasure—acting, as she did, as housekeeper, nurse, and governess. Go whenever you would into the house, you found Annie always busily engaged, and yet always in demand. From morning till night, from one quarter or the other, there was a call for Annie! So patiently, and so quietly, too, did she perform her multifarious duties, that it was really a pleasure to watch her movements. Captain and Mrs. Preston respected her; their children loved her tenderly; the male convicts on the estate obeyed her orders with cheerfulness, and the female convicts (this was, perhaps, the highest testimonial in her favour) abstained from reminding her that she was only their equal. As for the guests who were entertained by the Prestons, they not only admired Annie's pretty person and most decorous demeanour, but they envied the lady of the house and her extraordinary good fortunes. I need scarcely say that she was treated as a gentlewoman, who, when a young girl, had assisted in the commission of the greatest of all crimes under very peculiar if not extenuating circumstances, and whose conduct, apart from her crime, was entirely blameless. She did not, of course, sit at the same table with her employers (I cannot speak of them as master and mistress), but she had a room to herself, and seemingly comprehended her position so completely, that she was never guilty of the slightest encroachments.

After the birth of her eleventh child, Mrs. Preston had a very serious and painful illness. Annie tended her with all that care and affection of which her gentle nature was so capable; and, at the same time, kept the house quiet, the establishment in order; and Captain Preston's wants—he was selfish and exacting, though a well-bred man, and a perfect gentleman—ministered unto in every respect. But Mrs. Preston sank under her grievous malady—and died, to the great sorrow of every one who had enjoyed her acquaintance.

For a year after his wife's death Captain Preston never left his home—never went beyond the precincts of his own domain. But, at the expiration of that period, he paid us a visit, and as it was near our dinner hour, six o'clock, we invited him to stay and partake of the meal with us. He assented. We offered to send over a groom to his house to make known that he might not be expected until after ten or eleven. He replied that we need not do so, as he had intimated to Annie that he intended to stay the night at Macquarie Dale (such was the name of our estate). We were rejoiced to hear this, albeit there was something in Captain Preston's manner and discourse which betokened that he was very unquiet and unsettled in his mind.

During dinner, and for some time afterwards, the Captain was not only absent, silent, or incoherent when he spoke, but he glared occasionally at the Major and myself after a very odd and suspicious fashion. The dinner over, the cloth removed, and the dessert placed upon the table, our guest said that his object in paying us a visit that day was to impart some information, and that he hoped and trusted the course he was about to pursue would not involve the forfeiture of our friendship. 'You are aware,' proceeded Captain Preston, 'of the situation in which I was placed, when I had the misfortune to lose my wife, notwithstanding I could command the services of one on whom such implicit confidence could be placed. I allude of course to Annie Saint Felix. To all of my children, from my daughter, who is now verging into womanhood, down to the little one, which can scarcely walk alone, her behaviour has been such that my esteem and regard for her has at length resolved itself into an ardent affection. I love Annie Saint Felix, and if she will accept the offer I am about to make her, she shall become my wife. Yes, I will marry my bondswoman, for in strictness, that is her title. Whatever may be the opinion of the world I will brave it.'

'She is a worthy creature,' said the Major, heartily, 'and, with such a partner, there would be no particular valour in braving the opinion of the world. In the presence of my own wife, I desire to tell you, Preston, that, if I were in your position, my own feelings should be my sole counsellor.'

'You are silent,' said the Captain, addressing me, and placing his elbow on the table, he rested his head on the palm of his hand, his long brown hair standing out between his white and tapered fingers. He gazed at me very intently when he uttered those three words—'You are silent.'

'I was thinking,' I replied to him, in a solemn tone of voice, and meeting his gaze with one of equal intensity, 'of a scene which I should never have mentioned, or alluded to, had it not been for what you have just stated.'

'What scene?' he demanded, rather abruptly.

'A scene that occurred on the night which preceded that of your wife's death. I was with her, if you remember. Annie Saint Felix, worn out and exhausted by continual watching, had fallen asleep in the arm-chair. Your wife motioned me to place my ear to her lips. I did so. With an effort she raised her head from the pillow, fixed her eyes on the sleeping girl, and whispered to me, 'if my husband should ever think of marrying again, I hope that she will be his choice.' '

Captain Preston rose passionately from his chair, and grasped my hand. 'You have plucked from my mind the most anxious doubt that for several weeks past has literally haunted it. I have asked myself over and over again,— What would she have said?'

'Have you put the question to Miss Saint Felix?' the Major inquired.

'No,' said Captain Preston; 'but I will do so to-morrow.'

Annie at first objected to become the wife of Captain Preston, although she was very much attached to him. She was afraid that his union with her would prejudice his position in the colony, and eventually make him unhappy. But, at last, her scruples were overcome, and on one lovely winter's morning in the month of June, Captain Preston led Annie to the altar, where their hands were joined. The Major and myself, as well as those neighbours with whom we associated, were present; and, albeit the church in point of structure bore a very strong resemblance to an English barn, and there were no merry peals of bells, still there were joyous faces to greet the newly wedded pair when the ceremony concluded. They lived very happily together, and Annie became the mother of a little boy.

About eighteen months after this event Captain Preston unexpectedly inherited a large property in England. The amount of income may have been exaggerated; but rumour put it down at fifteen thousand pounds a-year. The Captain's presence was required in England, but he would not leave the colony until he could be accompanied by his wife. Remember that she was still a convict under sentence of transportation for the term of her natural life, though the most debased and brutal person in existence would never have dreamt of reminding her of that frightful fact.

It must have been a bitterly painful interview that which Captain Preston had with the governor of the colony; but it resulted in the removal of the obstacle which lay in the way of Annie's returning to Europe, and they left New South Wales to the very great regret of my husband and myself, and of many others.

The last time I saw Annie before she left the colony was in the streets of Sydney. She was leaning on the arm of her stepson, Charles Preston, who was then a tall youth of twenty years of age, and an ensign in a Regiment of Foot. He regarded his mother (as he always spoke of her) with a look so replete with filial affection,—spoke to her so kindly and so gently—seemed so proud of her (for she was still a very pretty woman) that my liking for him was far in excess of what it had been when he was only a boy.

Contributors to *Household Words*

The following biographical notes have quoted extensively from:
Anne Lohrli, *Household Words: A Weekly Journal 1850–1859, Conducted by Charles Dickens*, Toronto: University of Toronto Press, 1973. (Reprinted by permission, University of Toronto Press)

Other sources include:
Peter Ackroyd, *Dickens*, London: Mandarin Paperbacks, 1991.
Australian Dictionary of Biography 1851–1890, Vols. 1, 4 & 5, various eds., Melbourne: Melbourne University Press, 1959–76.
Tim Flannery, *The Birth of Melbourne*, Melbourne: Text Publishing, 2004
John Forster, *The Life of Charles Dickens: The Fireside Dickens*, London: Chapman and Hall Ltd. and Henry Frowde, c.1874.
Harry Gordon, *An Eyewitness History of Australia*, Melbourne: John Currey O'Neil, pp. 55–61, 1986.
Nancy Keesing, (Ed.), *History of the Australian Gold Rushes: By Those Who Were There*, Sydney: Angus & Robertson, Australia, 1987.
Mary Lazarus, *A Tale of Two Brothers: Charles Dickens's Sons in Australia*, Sydney: Angus & Robertson, 1973.
Una Pope-Hennessy, *Charles Dickens, 1812–1870*, London: The Reprint Society, 1947.
Harry Stone, *Charles Dickens' Uncollected Writings from Household Words 1850–1859*, Vols. 1 & 2, Bloomington, Indiana: University of Indiana Press, 1968.

Each entry finishes with the title(s) included in these volumes, with the volume number in parentheses; (1) *Convict Stories*, (2) *Immigration*, (3) *Frontier Stories*, (4) *Mining and Gold* (5) *Maritime Conditions*.

Anonymous, payment for the item listed below (*H.W.* Office Book) was made to Robert Bell an intimate friend of Dickens. Bell had provided to the editorial office a letter written to him from a friend in Australia. It was dated 25 December 1850 and from North Kapunda, South Australia.[1]
– 'Life in the Burra Mines of South Australia' (4).

Anonymous (no payment recorded). In the article the contributor explains how two persons, 'fighting fire with fire' can, 'with perfect ease,' contain and control a bush fire.
– 'Chip: The Bush-Fire Extinguisher', W.H. Wills & a correspondent (3).

Capper, John (1814–1898). Capper was a resident of Ceylon (Sri Lanka) who worked as a journalist covering events in Ceylon and India for forty years. He was a correspondent for the London *Times* and also a regular contributor to *H.W.* Nearly sixty of his articles were published in *H.W.* between March 1851 and March, 1858.

Capper was the author of many books on Australia: *Perils, Pastimes, and Pleasures of an Emigrant in Australia; The Emigrants' Guide to Australia*, 1852; and also, *Australia: As a Field for Capital, Skill, and Labour*, 1854. In addition, he recorded himself on the title pages of two of his books as the author of 'Our Gold Colonies' and on the title page of another, as author of the 'Gold Fields'.
– 'Off to the Diggings!' (5); 'First Stage to Australia', Capper & W.H. Wills (2); 'The Great Screw' [Screw Propeller] (5).

Chisholm, Caroline (1808–1877) was born in England. From 1832 to 1838 her husband, Captain Archibald, was stationed in Madras. It was there she began a lifelong career as a passionate social activist establishing a school for the neglected children of soldiers.

She came to Australia on leave in 1836, and remained in Sydney after her husband's recall to active service (1840–45), to continue her work protecting poor working women. She established the Female Emigrants' Home in Sydney in 1841 and conducted groups of immigrant women into the interior. This was done both to safeguard them and to find them suitable situations.

She met every immigrant ship, and as a result, founded the Registry Office for Immigrant Families. While in Australia she published *Female Immigration Considered* (1842), describing her activities in the Female Emigrants' Home.

After her husband's retirement in 1845 he joined her in collecting information from over 600 immigrants about their experiences in Australia. This was later to serve as a guide for future immigrants. On their return to England (1846–54), the Chisholm's worked to assist immigrants and helped the wives and children of liberated convicts, then in Australia, to migrate to join their husbands. In 1849 she established The Family Colonization Loan Society to enable the poor to migrate to Australia. Chisholm wrote pamphlets on immigration and wrote letters to influential persons seeking assistance for her projects, as well as supervising the passage of immigrant ships.[2]

On 24 February 1850, Elizabeth Herbert, the wife of Dickens' friend Sydney Herbert (who financially supported both Chisholm's and Dickens' humanitarian work), wrote to Mrs Chisholm:

> I saw Mr. Dickens to-day and he has commissioned me to say that if you will allow him, and unless he hears to the contrary from you, he will call upon you at 2 o'clock on Tuesday next, the 26th ... I told him about your emigrants' letter, and he seemed to think that giving them publicity would be an important engine towards helping in our work, and he has so completely the confidence of the lower classes (who all read his Books if they can read at all) that I think if you can persuade him to bring them out in his new work it will be an immense step gained.[3]

This timely meeting of Chisholm with Dickens seems to have influenced his attitude to Australia—well beyond the articles published in her name. Her 'emigrants' letters' appeared in the first number of Dickens' 'new work'. When writing to Wills on March 6, 1850, Dickens mentioned 'A Bundle of Emigrants' Letters' as 'a little article of my own ... introducing five or six originals [letters], which are extremely good. Dickens paid tribute to, and endorsed, Mrs Chisholm's work[4] thus providing powerful aid, publicity and credibility to her work.

When her husband returned to Australia in 1851 to continue their work, she remained in England until 1854. It was during this time that amendments to the Passenger Act (1852) to improve conditions aboard migrant ships took effect. The new regulations were largely due to the Chisholms' advocacy.

Six articles written for *H.W.* from 1850 to 1852 promoted her work. Two were by W.H. Wills, 'Safety for Female Emigrants' and 'Official Emigration'. The others were by Samuel Sidney, 'Two Scenes of the Life of John Bodger', 'Three Colonial Epochs', 'Better Ties than Red Tape' and 'What to Take to Australia'. Sidney also referred to Mrs Chisholm's work in his book *Emigrant's Journal*.

After returning to Australia (1854) she toured the goldfields to assess conditions for travellers and this resulted in ten shelter sheds being built on the routes to the diggings. She lobbied government to assist settlers to gain small land holdings and reform land administration.[5] The Chisholms returned to England in 1866. In recognition of her service to immigrants her portrait was placed on the first issued series of the Australian five-dollar note (1966).

– 'A Bundle of Emigrants' Letters', Charles Dickens & Caroline Chisholm (2); 'Pictures of Life in Australia', Charles Dickens & Caroline Chisholm (2).

Cox, Miss (no first name recorded) whose address was noted as Kensington. The article 'Easy Spelling and Hard Reading' reproduces the letter of a barely literate Englishman who had emmigrated to Australia. W.H. Wills (*H.W.* editor, see below) was probably responsible for the introductory comments in the article which criticised the 'want of national means of education' in England, as a result the son of poor parents grew up without the schooling that would make him 'a literate and useful citizen'. This was one of many articles on education published in *H.W.* decrying the lack of education for the masses.

– 'Chip: Easy Spelling and Hard Reading', Miss Cox & W.H. Wills (2).

Dickens, Charles (1812–1870). Journalist, editor, novelist and accomplished stage performer. He wrote fourteen novels. As a boy Dickens worked for five months in a blacking factory while his family was in debtor's prison. This experience had a powerful influence on his thinking for the remainder of his life. His writing career started when he was employed as an office boy in an attorney's office. After learning shorthand Dickens became an expert parliamentary and court reporter, as well as general reporter of the *Mirror of Parliament*; *True Sun* and the *Morning Chronicle*. As a young man he contributed sketches to *Monthly Chronicle*; *Evening Chronicle* and *Bell's Life in London*.

Throughout his highly productive career Dickens was primarily a journalist, always seeking to promote social change and awareness. He established several publications: *Daily News* (1846); *Household Words* (1850–1859); and *All the Year Round* (1859–1870). In January 1850, two months before *H.W.* was first published Dickens began *Household Narrative of Current Events*. It was a monthly supplement of news[6] supplying condensed reports of proceedings in parliament as well as chronicling the principal lawsuits and articles on important books. There were no editorial or other comments. It also included statistics on crime, accidents and disasters, social, sanitary and municipal progress, obituaries, colonies and dependencies, foreign events, literature and arts, commercial records, stocks and share, and emigration figures.

Dickens seems to have had a fascination with Australia. According to his friend and biographer John Forster, during the 1850s he had a 'recurring notion' about emigrating,[7] (which was more likely a fantasy than a serious consideration). Even so, in 1862 he did seriously contemplate a trip to Australia when offered £10,000 to perform his readings,[8] (and this provides an indication of his popularity in Australia).

Two of Dickens' children migrated to Australia. Alfred (1845–1912) arrived in 1865, receiving assistance from Sir Archibald Michie (see below). He became a stock and station agent in the Western Districts of Victoria before moving to Melbourne in 1882. Alfred returned to England in 1910. Edward (1852–1905) came to Australia at the age of sixteen (in 1869) and lived in Western NSW for over thirty years. For a time he owned a station near Bourke, later working at the Lands Office in Moree and briefly represented Wilcannia in the NSW Legislative Assembly. Dickens maintained a correspondence with his sons in Australia until his death in 1870.[9]

Dickens wrote or co-wrote nearly 200 articles for *H.W.* including prose and verse, as well as novels printed in instalments, such as *Hard Times*. He received £500 per annum for his work on *H.W.* plus a share of the profits.
– 'A Bundle of Emigrants' Letters', Charles Dickens & Mrs Chisholm (2); 'Pictures of Life in Australia', Charles Dickens & Mrs Chisholm (2); 'Chip: Fine Art in Australia' (2); 'Home for Homeless Women' (2).

Fawkner, John Pascoe (1792–1869) a correspondent and pioneer settler in Australia, especially of Melbourne. Born in London, Fawkner had received only a few years schooling. His father was sentenced to transportation but was permitted to take his family with him when dispatched from England in April 1803. Until October 1835, John Fawkner had various occupations, mainly in Van Diemen's Land, from where he arranged an expedition to Port Phillip for the purpose of establishing a farm on the northern side of the Yarra (with 500 sheep and fifty cattle). The settlement ultimately became Melbourne.

In 1838 Fawkner founded the *Melbourne Advertiser*, the first newspaper in Victoria, followed by the *Port Phillip Patriot*. He took an active role in matters relating to governing Victoria, both before and after separation from NSW in 1851. Fawkner held various official posts and served in the Victorian legislature for eighteen years.

Fawkner's pioneering work in Port Phillip received mention in *H.W.* in Howitt's 'The Old and New Squatter', 8 December, 1855. The article published in *H.W.* entitled 'A Colonial Patriot' was a letter to Dickens from Fawkner and not intended for publication. In the letter he wrote: 'I pray you to pardon this liberty, but I could not refrain from thanking you for the very favourable manner in which my conduct has been reported in your journal'. He stated that he had almost all of Dickens' work as well as *H.W.* and Dickens' monthly periodical, *Household Narrative of Current Events*.[10]
– 'Chip: A Colonial Patriot', Fawkner & Howitt (3).

Gill, Charles (contributor not identified). The introduction to the item states that the 'contributor is an Englishman for six years resident in Victoria.' Gill's article discusses the climate of Victoria and also contains a reference to the huge bush fire of 1851, 'already described in this Journal' (Black Thursday, of May 10, 1856 written by William Howitt).
– 'Sultry December' (2).

Gwynne, Francis squatter and landowner in NSW who migrated to Australia (date uncertain). In partnership with his brothers Richard and Henry, Francis took up Crown Lands outside the 'Limits of Location'. The Gwynne brothers were recorded as being the holders of the Barratta cattle station, north of the Edward River, in the Murrumbidgee squatting district, which they held until 1853. Henry then took over Werai station and Francis bought Murgah station, adjoining Barratta to the west, with 750 cattle for £6750, which he sold in 1872. In the 1860s he was a JP in the Moulamein district.[11]

The two letters that constitute the article were addressed by the writer to 'a relative in Cheshire,' apparently another brother, William. Gwynne's letter records raids by 'blacks' on the Gwynne's cattle and attacks on the Gwynne's two stations. *H.W.* published the letters to 'furnish some idea of how new localities are colonised by such enterprising pioneers as the writer.'
– 'Two Letters from Australia', Francis Gwynne & W.H. Wills (3).

Hill, Catherine (correspondent not identified). Hill was referred to in an editorial comment as a 'correspondent in Adelaide, Australia.'
– 'Chip: Hornet Architecture', (2).

Hogarth, Jr (identity uncertain), thought to be a son of George Hogarth who was part of Dickens' circle of friends and is recorded as having had five sons and five daughters. George Hogarth was a lawyer, music critic and journalist who contributed four articles to *Household Words*.

Little is known about the contributor of the articles listed below. The details that accompanied them, (which are unconfirmed) stated that the contributor had migrated to Australia before the goldrush at 'the beginning of the winter of 1850 and was working quietly in Sydney, [and] by no means dissatisfied with his position.' When rumours of Bathurst gold reached the city, Hogarth resigned his position and advertised in the *Sydney Morning Herald* for 'a gentleman, willing to join him and share the expenses of going to Turon diggings.' He chose as partner one of the men who answered his advertisement and proceeded with him to the diggings. He was there (unsuccessfully) for about four months (see, 'Cradle and the Grave')[12]

Hogarth co-authored two articles for *Household Words*—one in conjunction with Richard Horne and another with Joseph Morley (see biographies below).

– 'Chip: Look Before You Leap', R.H. Horne & Hogarth Jr (2); 'The Cradle and the Grave', Hogarth Jr. & Morley (presumably, Joseph) (2).

Horne, Richard Henry (or Hengist) (1802–1884), was a London-born author who was educated at Sandhurst. He had a life full of adventure which included 'a tour in the Mexican navy, pitched battles, an encounter with a shark, yellow fever, shipwreck, mutiny, and fire at sea; as well as exploits with Indians in the U.S.A.' He produced poems, plays, travel narratives, novels, biographies, children's stories and various articles on a huge range of subjects. Horne met Dickens in the 1830s and they became good friends with much in common. In 1841 Horne served on royal commission on child employment in factories.[13]

From the commencement of publication of *H.W.* in 1850, Horne was one of the early salaried members of the staff receiving £250 per annum, (half the rate of Dickens' own salary). He wrote original prose and poetry, revised contributed articles, and assisted Wills in editing the journal.

Horne travelled to Australia (arriving in September 1852) in the company of William Howitt, having agreed to supply *H.W.* with a number of travel pieces in return for advances to equip the expedition and for regular payments to his wife.[14]

Horne remained in Australia for seventeen years, returning to England in 1869. While in Australia he had a varied career. He became commander of a private gold escort and in 1853, assistant gold commissioner at Heathcote and Waranga until 1854.[15] He was employed as a clerk for Sir Archibald Michie (see below) a commissioner of sewerage and water, as well as standing unsuccessfully for a seat in parliament in 1857. Horne was an active member of Melbourne's Garrick Club. He wrote a satirical piece about the club whose members went on to perform it.[16] On his return to England in 1869, Dickens refused to have anything to do with him because he had contributed little to Mrs Horne's support during his time in Australia.

He wrote sixty-nine articles for *H.W.* (twelve of which related to Australia) and twenty-four poems. During his career he published many books of prose and poetry, including a book for potential migrants, *Australian Facts and Prospects*, London, 1859. In 1874 Horne was granted a pension of £50 per annum in recognition of his services to literature.

– 'Pictures of Life in Australia', Caroline Chisholm & Horne (2); 'A Digger's Diary', [in 4 parts] (4); 'Chip: Look Before You Leap', Horne & Hogarth Jr. (2); 'Gentlemen and Bullocks' (3); 'Canvass Town [sic]' (2); 'Chip: Digging Sailors' (4); 'Chip: A Digger's Wedding' (4); 'Convicts in the Gold Region' (1).

Howitt, William (1792–1879) received his education at a Quaker school. He was self-taught in languages, chemistry, botany, natural science and dispensing of medicines. He became writer and is credited with 180 publications. Along with his wife Mary (who contributed three prose articles and seven items of verse) he was a regular contributor to *Household Words*. The Howitts were great admirers of Dickens' writings, particularly because of the couple's social awareness and advocacy for reform.

Due to financial need, at the age of sixty, William Howitt sailed to Australia in the company of Richard Horne, along with Howitt's two sons— Alfred William (known as William, 1830–1909) and Charlton. Howitt's younger brothers Godfrey (1800–1873) a physician and natural scientist and Richard (1799–1870) a poet, had preceded them to Port Phillip in 1840.

When Howitt arrived in Melbourne he already had a reputation as an author and poet. While in Australia he wrote many articles describing in detail aspects of life and work at the diggings.[17] His accounts were acknowledged for their 'objectivity and tolerance'.[18]

Howitt travelled to the goldfields with his sons at intervals during the two years and discovered the rich Nine-Mile-Creek diggings, where he was moderately successful.[19] He was said to have revelled in bush life and the

163

strange flora and fauna. He recognised the necessity to reform the land laws and also offered sensible suggestions for improvement in the gold commissioners 'comic opera' police force. His advice was ignored. Howitt returned to England in 1854.

His son Alfred William elected to stay in Australia where he initially farmed at his uncle's farm in Caulfield, and later had interests were pastoral stations at Yea and Cape Schanck.[20] His brother Charlton went to New Zealand in 1860 where he worked as a surveyor. Alfred William was to become a leading explorer and led a party to find and later retrieve the remains of Burke and Wills. He was a natural scientist and pioneer and an authority on Aboriginal culture and social organisation. He was acknowledged by Sir Baldwin Spencer for laying down the foundations of the scientific study of Aborigines. He became a drover, police magistrate, goldfields warden and secretary for mines. Alfred William was a prolific writer, especially about the Victorian goldfields.[21]

It is reasonable to assume that Howitt maintained a correspondence with his sons long after his return to England, thus keeping him, and his circle, informed about current events in Australia.

Other publications by William Howitt include: *A Boys Adventure in the Wilds of Australia*, 1854; *Land Labour and Gold, or Two Years in Victoria*, (London: Longmans, 1855); *Tasmania and New Zealand*, 1856. His articles in the book were published first in *Household Words* and later reproduced as interpolated stories in *Tallangetta: the Squatter's Home*, (by William Howitt). Two Vols, London: Longman, Brown, Green, Longmans and Roberts, 1857 (publication in *H.W.* acknowledged).[22]

– 'The Old and New Squatter' (3); 'The Landlord' (3); 'Black Thursday' (3); 'Gold Hunting in Two Parts' (4); 'The Land Shark' (3).

Irwin, Mr (not identified) In the item below, Irwin mentions having been to Norfolk Island. He wrote, 'I know the place well and the people living there, convicts and all. How I came by my knowledge is a question which I am not obliged to answer; but, for the comfort of the clean-fingered, I am not legally pitch.' A further article, 'Caught in a Typhoon', was published in *H.W.* in 1853, where Irwin recounted a stormy passage on board ship from Macau to Singapore.[23] He wrote two further articles about Australia in 1853 and 1854. In the *Geelong Advertiser* in December 1854 there was an item covering the Eureka Stockade by a Samuel Irwin, who was 'regarded as one of the most responsible eyewitnesses and his very full and accurate report of the incident,'[24] some of which was used in government dispatches to the Secretary for the Colony about the affair. During the same period he is recorded as being the editor of the *Ballarat Star*. Whether Mr Irwin (above) and Samuel Irwin were the same person has not been confirmed.

– 'Norfolk Island', Irwin & Henry Morley (1); 'Chip: Sentimental Geography' (5); 'Chip: The Antecedents of Australia' (1).

Keene, William Thomas (1798–1872). William Keene's brothers, John and James (of Kingsmead Street, Bath), were commercial printers and proprietors of *Keene's Bath Journal*, founded 1744.[25] The *Sydney Morning Herald*'s and additional information supporting the article was supplied to Wills (Dickens editor) by one of William's brothers.

William Keene emmigrated to Victoria in the early 1850's later moving with his family to NSW. He had studied medicine in London, and later geology and engineering, working as a mining engineer and civil engineer in Bordeaux France in the 1830's. Keene completed a geological survey of the Fitzroy iron mines near Mittagong, and in 1854 was appointed Examiner of Coalfields. He remained principally in NSW and in the 1860's worked on the coal-bearing rocks and oil shale in the Sydney Basin.

His geological reports were published principally in government gazettes and some in newspapers. He is remembered for his work on coal deposits and the water supply of the area, and for providing geological material for exhibition in London, Paris and Melbourne as well as to collectors around the world. William Keene was a member of the Geological Society of London where he published two articles in *Quarterly Journal*.[26] He also served as a magistrate for a short time.

– 'Chip: A Golden Newspaper', William Keene & William Wills (4).

Lang, John (1816–1864) barrister, journalist, novelist. He was born in Parramatta, NSW the son of Walter Lang, a merchant adventurer who married Elizabeth Harris, the Australian born daughter of First Fleeter John Harris. Lang was educated at Sydney College and Trinity College Cambridge. He studied law and was called to the bar in 1838 and in 1839 returned to Sydney. In 1843 he left Sydney for Calcutta where he lived for most of the remainder of his life. In India, Lang founded and edited the newspaper *The Moffussilite*, and later, for a time edited the *Optimist* in Meerut. He devoted most of his time to literary works while contributing to several publications. Lang wrote twenty novels, most of which were published anonymously in *The Moffussilite*.

John Lang published several books relating to Australia including *The Forger's Wife*, which is almost identical to his 'Charles Fredrick Howard', a story in *Legends of Australia*, (1842) which he published anonymously. He also published *Botany Bay: or True Tales of Early Australia* (1859), a collection of short sketches and stories (thinly disguised as fiction) of events and people in the convict period.[27] Lang's books were very popular.

He wrote twenty-four articles for *H.W.* the ones listed below, together with five additional stories were later published as *Botany Bay*, by John Lang, Esq., Barrister at Law, London: William Tegg, 1859, (publication in *H.W.* acknowledged). *Botany Bay* was frequently reprinted. These included *Clever Criminals* and *Remarkable Convicts*. A Melbourne edition (reprinting only ten of the thirteen stories that constituted the book) was titled *Fisher's Ghost and Other Stories of the Early Days of Australia*.[28]
– 'Fisher's Ghost' (3); 'Tracks in the Bush' (3); 'An Illustrious British Exile' (1); 'A Special Convict' (1); 'Baron Wald' (1); 'Three Celebrities' (1); 'Kate Crawford' (1); 'Miss Saint Felix' (1).

Macpherson, Ossian (contributor not identified) published four articles in *Household Words*. Three printed in 1851 dealt with the writer's interest in improving social conditions and redressing common social abuses. 'The Smithfield Model' concerns the removal of the filthy, unhygienic Smithfield cattle market from the centre of the City of London (and other towns and cities). 'A Few Facts about Salt' denounces the 'odious imposition' of government tax on Indian salt and the injustice done to the natives. 'Excursion Trains' calls for railway companies to institute cheap fares for patrons by showing the benefit to the owners themselves.[29]

The fourth article on Australia, written in 1852, in conjunction with Morley and Mulock in this collection, is titled 'The Harvest of Gold', is attributed to the same author. Although not dealing specifically with social need, it relates the history of the discovery of gold in Australia and detailed conditions in the goldfields as recorded in newspapers and also, in letters from immigrants such as Mulock (see below). It also discusses the economic effects on Britain should a decrease in the value of gold occur as a result of finding it in Australia. The discussion about the decrease in the value of gold was probably the writing of Morley (see below), who dealt with that matter in an article in the following month.
– 'The Harvest of Gold' (4).

Marryatt, Miss (contributor uncertain). Frederick Marryatt was a friend of Dickens. They met socially and sometimes corresponded with each other. His daughters were all writers. Two, Augusta and Emilia wrote stories with Australia as a setting. 'Friends in Australia' is about an Englishman who takes a voyage to Australia for the sake of his health. The story records a horseback trip in New South Wales, and some incidents, 'for the most part true,' related by the Englishman's friend of his experiences in Australia 'twenty years ago, less or more.' There is no suggestion that the writer had any personal experience of Australia.
– 'Friends in Australia' (3).

Meredith, Louisa Anne (Twarmley) (1812–1895) was born near Birmingham. She published poems and at least twenty-three books, many with illustrations that she had designed and etched herself. Louisa was fearless as an author; she wrote on social and religious issues, and published several newspaper articles in support of Chartists.[30] In 1839 she married Charles Meredith, a squatter from New South Wales and, in the same year, accompanied him to Sydney, and later to Tasmania, where she remained for the rest of her life. For the fifty years she lived in Australia, Meredith recorded colonial life in NSW, Victoria and Tasmania.

She became interested in politics, and wrote unsigned articles for Tasmanian newspapers and contributed to *Australian Ladies' Annual*, in addition to sending occasional articles to British periodicals, including *Household Words*. Meredith wrote seventeen books, including *Notes and Sketches of New South Wales* (1844). At least nine of her books written in either prose form or poetry, related to Tasmania and many were illustrated. She was passionate about the protection of native wildlife and wrote many books describing Tasmanian flowers and insects, with the descriptions interspersed with verses and illustrated colour plates from her drawings. These included *Some of My Bush Friends in Australia* (1860) and a second series of *Bush Friends* which were published in 1891. She also wrote *Tasmanian Friends and Foes; Feathered, Furred and Finned* (in story form); *Grandmamma's Verse Book for Young Australia*; and, *Waratah Rhymes for Young Australia* and other books.[31]

After her husband's death in 1880 Meredith was granted a pension of £100 per annum by the Tasmanian government in recognition to her work in literature, art and science.[32]

– 'The Shadows of the Golden Image' (4); 'Little Bell' (3).

Michie, Sir Archibald (1810–1899), English born jurist and statesman. He studied law and was called to the bar in 1838 and also worked as a journalist for the *Atlas* newspaper.

He migrated to Sydney in 1839 to practise law and in May 1841 was admitted to the NSW Barrister Roll. He sailed to South Australia in 1847 and in the same year a publication containing a two page preface by Michie, about the *Case of Mr. W.H. Barber* ... (a convicted convict, later established as innocent), was printed.[33] Following his return to Sydney from South Australia, Michie was endorsed by the Anti-Transportation League for the Legislative Council seat of Cumberland County in 1849, but was unsuccessful.

He then returned to England arriving soon after W. H. Barber, (himself a lawyer and now pardoned) had published a book about his case. Barber's book and Michie's arrival in England coincided with the publication of *Household Words* and it is likely that this is when the articles listed below were written. Dickens was interested in the issue of Barber as he had a copy of Barbers book in his library.[34] In July and August of this same year Dickens published Barber's story in *H.W.* as 'Transported for Life: In Two Parts', (reprinted in Book 1) with Barber's name withheld. These articles were written by William Thomas (see biography below).

About 1852 Michie left England for Canada, then proceeded to Sydney and finally settled in Melbourne where he practised law. He was admitted to serve in the Victorian Supreme Court and later (1863) became Victoria's first QC. In 1856 he was elected to the new Victorian Legislative Council. He was twice attorney-general and was minister for justice and later, for six years, agent-general for Victoria in London. He was made a K.C.M.G., and returned to Melbourne on his retirement. He was regarded as having a brilliant legal mind and is remembered as one of the barristers who defended the Eureka Rebels (1855).[35]

It is highly probable Michie met Dickens while in England and it is known that Dickens corresponded with him in Australia. One of Dickens' letters referred to *H.W.* writer Richard Horne (see above) whom Michie had employed as a clerk in his office. Dickens recalled seeing Horne invent 'an immense corkscrew', before he left England; it was to be used for the 'infallible' extraction of gold with which he expected to make his fortune at the diggings.[36] In contrast, when Dickens wrote to Horne about Michie (1865), he declared his 'appreciation of Michie's kindness to young Alfred Dickens, who had migrated to Australia in May of that year.'[37]

Michie was a distinguished speaker and lecturer, and several of his addresses were published as pamphlets. He wrote for *Melbourne Herald*, *Punch* and for many years was the Victorian correspondent for *The Times*.[38]

Michie's name did not appear in items listed below. In the first, (written in conjunction with Morley) the writer identified himself as one of the 'London barristers' in Sydney and states that his 'own diggings' were in the Supreme Court. He records a trip to Maitland related to the assize held there.

He describes Sydney as he saw the city on his first arrival and as he came to know it, 'a subsequent nine years' experience.'[39]

– 'Going Circuit at the Antipodes', Michie & Morley (1); 'Chip: A Visit to the Burra Burra Mines' (4).

Morley, Henry (1822–1892), the archetypical 'Man of Letters' was educated in England at King's College, London, in the faculty of arts and medicine and also in Germany. He practised medicine for four years and then for two years conducted his own school. From 1851 to 1865 Morley served on the staff of *H.W.* and *All the Year Round*. He was appointed professor of English language and literature at University College from 1865 to 1889 and held other academic appointments.

Morley's friendship with Dickens developed through his involvement with *H.W.* Lohrli records that 'in a letter of 1850, Morley expressed great admiration for Dickens' writing; opining that Dickens lacked 'sound literary taste … his own genius, brilliant as it is, appears often in a dress which shows that he has more heart and wit than critical refinement'; a conviction that was to remain long after Dickens' death.[40] Also that Morley's connection to *H.W.* resulted from Dickens' interest in certain papers on sanitation and health that he had written. Two of the papers, published in *Journal of Public Health*, had been reprinted in newspapers. Dickens' request that Morley might write for *H.W.* on matters of sanitation was enclosed in a letter from Forster, a lawyer, and close friend of Dickens.

Initially Morley was not enthusiastic about writing for *H.W.* because the audience he would be writing for was distinctly low-brow—as according to him, his usual audience in comparison was 'clever, liberal-minded and loved wit'. However he agreed to do so. Morley wrote, 'but for the sake of making Dickens' acquaintance … and having 'a second pulpit to preach health'. Initially he found it difficult to find the right style to communicate with his new audience. He wrote on many topics, especially those related to health, including sanitation, medicine and scientific matters, conditions in factories (that drew the wrath of factory-owners), life on board ships, mines, schooling and other social conditions. Some of his articles were rejected by Dickens, some rewritten and others returned for revision.[41]

In 1851 Morley was offered a salaried position on *H.W.* at £5 per week and was the only university-educated staff member. In that capacity, to use his own words, 'to act as a sort of deputy-lieutenant, writing papers of my own, revising or rewriting any paper found in the letter-box that contained matter useful to the public, that was ill-written or ill-arranged, and making myself generally useful'.

Morley wrote 382 prose article and five poems for *Household Words*. Four of his poems were reprinted in *Gossip*. He also contributed articles to many literary journals. He was the author of books of poems, fairy tales, numerous biographies, as well as ten volumes on English writers. In the latter part of his life, he edited some 300 volumes of English and foreign classics. Morley wrote, or co-wrote twelve articles for *H.W.*, that related to Australia, (listed below) and co-wrote one relating to New Zealand.

– 'Going Circuit at the Antipodes', Michie & Morley (1); 'A Rainy Day on the 'Euphrates'' (2); 'Norfolk Island', Irwin & Morley (1); 'The Harvest of Gold' Morley, Macpherson & Mulock (4); 'Chip: Highland Emigration' (2); 'Sailors' Home Afloat' (5); 'We Mariners of England' (5); 'Bad Luck at Bendigo', Henry & Joseph Morley (4); 'Among the Shallows' (1); 'The Cradle and the Grave', Hogarth Jr & Morley (4); 'Chip: Voices from the Deep', Morley & an anonymous contributor (5); 'John Chinaman in Australia' (2); 'Britannia's Figures' (2).

Morley, Joseph (1816– date not known) was Henry Morley's brother. Joseph was more conventional and conservative than his younger brother Henry.

According to Joseph Morley's article in *H.W.*, he went to Australia in 1849 (prior to the Victorian gold discoveries) and found, on his arrival, that the letters of introduction he had been given to influential people in Melbourne were of no value as people in Melbourne 'received a great many more drafts upon their courtesy than they could possibly honour.' When gold was found, he decided, with some of his shipmates to try his luck at the diggings. He was unsuccessful and soon returned to England.[42]

– 'Bad Luck at Bendigo', Henry & Joseph Morley (4).

Mr Mulock (not identified). The first and third items listed below are letters (or extracts from letters) that were written by a contributor in 1851, from Geelong to a friend in England. According to the letters and the editorial remarks accompanying them, the contributor was a young man who was a 'recent settler' in Australia.[43] The article states that in partnership with Mr Rumble, he had bought a farm near Mt Swardle (or Swaddle [sic]), an extinct volcano in the Geelong district, described as being a thousand years old. Recent investigations reveal no records of a Mt Swardle (or Swaddle) in the district, or of this name having been used in the past and, according to Assoc. Prof. E.B. Joyce, from the School of Earth Sciences, Melbourne University, the area has many extinct volcanoes, all older than those described in the article.[44]

Lohrli's research indicated that payment for the third item listed as 'handed by Wills,' July 10, was presumably to Mulock's correspondent. It is possible that the noted author and poet, Dinah Maria Mulock, who also contributed to *H. W.*, may have been the person responsible for providing the letters.

– 'Chip: A Bush Fire in Australia' (3); 'The Harvest of Gold' (4); 'We, and Our Man Tom' (2).

Ollier, Edmund (1827–1886) a writer and poet, was the son of Charles Ollier, the prominent publisher of poets such as Keats and Shelley. Edmund Ollier had acted in an editorial capacity at *Leader, Atlas* and *London Review* and as a contributor to several periodicals.[45]

He wrote to Dickens in 1850, some ten weeks prior to commencement of the publication of *H. W.*, to ask about the possibility of writing for the new periodical. Dickens' reply suggested that he would not 'pledge himself beforehand, to the acceptance of any article' but that the plans for the 'projected Miscellany' called for the use of good occasional contributions.[46] Ollier contributed fifteen prose pieces to *H.W.* and a further thirty-four poems. It would appear that Ollier's work was 'well appreciated by the illustrious conductor' and in 1852, Dickens himself wrote of Ollier being 'an excellent and true young poet.'[47]

Ollier wrote one poem in relation to Australia, 'The Ballad of the Gold Digger'. This was published at the time when many articles focusing on Australia, particularly on the gold diggings, were being printed in *H.W.* from contributors such as Horne, Hogarth, Michie, Mulock, and Sidney.
– 'The Ballad of the Gold Digger' (4).

Payn, James (1830–1898) was a noted English novelist. Payn was educated at Eton, The Royal Military Academy, Woolwich and Cambridge University. While still an undergraduate Payn started sending verse and prose to periodicals and also published two volumes of verse. He became a close friend of Dickens, and they exchanged many letters. Lohrli states that he was obviously a great admirer of Dickens as his letters made frequent reference to him. She noted that Payn had written that Dickens 'wrote letters as good as his books.'[48] Payn wrote sixty-seven prose articles and one poem for *Household Words*. His article 'The Savage Muse' was a scathing, almost sarcastic criticism of a hugely popular 'poetical narrative' of Kinahan Cornwallis that was in vogue at the time. Cornwallis (1839–1917) had spent time working in Melbourne as a public servant leaving Australia in 1855. He also published prose articles about Melbourne.[49]

According to Payn's article, Cornwallis' poem 'Yarra Yarra, or the Wandering Aborigine', was in thirteen books and in its fifth edition. In the long narrative poem, to which Payn took exception, Cornwallis had apparently professed to detail the life of an Australian Aborigine named Yarra Yarra. Payn deplored Cornwallis' idealised depiction of the Aboriginal, referring to it as 'the noble savage, with a vengeance.' About the time Payn's piece was printed in the periodical Dickens published various others describing experiences with Aborigines (he too was not an admirer of the concept of the noble savage.) The name 'The Savage Muse' has a typical Dickensian title, being a double or, even triple pun.
– 'The Savage Muse' (3).

Rinder, Samuel (1825–1907), businessman and public official in Victoria. Rinder was the son of a Methodist preacher, and was born and educated in Leeds. There is some confusion in relation to his early life history.[50] As a boy

Rinder went to sea as a cabin boy on a vessel sailing between Liverpool and New York. In the early 1840s he was an apprentice on the *Hope of Plymouth*. He sailed to Melbourne and stayed for some years in Tasmania with an uncle. About 1849, he returned to England, having sailed via Peru with the intention of getting to California where gold had recently been found; stayed for about three years, then shipped out again to Melbourne where he started a butcher's business. He then worked for two years carting goods between Melbourne and the Castlemaine diggings. Ever resourceful, Rinder operated a general store, became a grazier, farmer and finally a leading businessman in the Korong district. He was secretary and treasurer of the Korong Shire for forty years and a justice of the peace.

Rinder was an able writer and speaker. In addition to contributing to Victorian newspapers, he wrote eight articles for *H.W.* between 1852 and 1855, five of which related to Australia. Of the eight, Rinder was recorded in five as the sole writer. In the remaining three he wrote in conjunction with Morley. His description of whaling in 'Black Skin A-head!' reads as a first hand narrative that stands the test of time as a descriptive piece. 'We Mariners of England' and 'Sailor's Home Afloat' draw attention to and sharply criticises, the poor working conditions endured by sailors on board English vessels. The criticisms made in 'Sailors Home Afloat', was confirmed in a follow-up letter (published anonymously as a Chip) from 'a master mariner of the Antipodes' in *Voices from the Deep* (reprinted in Book 5).
– 'Black-Skin Ahead!' (5); 'Sailors' Home Afloat' (5); 'We Mariners of England' Rinder & Morley (5); 'Four-Legged Australians' (2); 'Australian Carriers' (4); 'Chip: Voices from the Deep' (5).

Sala, George Augustus Henry Fairfield (1828–1895) was educated in France and England. He was a journalist, essayist, lecturer and editor. From a family of singers and actors, Sala initially earned a living as a scene painter, illustrator and engraver. He met Dickens in 1836 when his mother acted in one of Dickens' plays and, with a 'precocious talent' for writing and drawing, entered early into the London literary society.[51]

In the 1840's Sala started contributing to minor London journals, and in 1851 began writing articles for Dickens' *Household Words*. Dickens' biographer John Forster relates that Sala was regarded by Dickens at the 'highest ranks' to assist him,[52] and as such in 1856, Dickens sent him to Russia to write a number of travel sketches. He wrote nearly 150 articles for *H.W.*, of which two were related to Australia. After a disagreement with Dickens in 1857, Sala started a long association with the *Daily Telegraph* and was sent by the paper to New York, Europe and elsewhere around the globe, including Australia. Sala also published some forty works of fiction and non-fiction—he was a highly entertaining and prolific writer, with a worldwide reputation. After reconciling with Dickens, he later wrote for *All the Year Round*.

Sala visited Melbourne in the 1885. It was he who coined the name 'Marvellous Melbourne', to capture the wealth and excitement of the city for his newspaper readers in England.[53]

– 'Cheerily, Cheerily!' (2); 'Unfortunate James Daley' (4).

Sidney, John (1821–?), son of physician, Abraham Solomon, and like his brother Samuel, (below) adopted the anglicised surname 'Sidney'. Having completed his education in France and England, John Sidney, at the age of seventeen in 1838, arrived in New South Wales where he raised sheep, cattle and horses in the 'wildest parts of the colony'. He stayed in Australia for six years, leaving for England in 1844.

In 1847, Smith Elder and Co. published, *A Voice from the Far Interior of Australia, By a Bushman*, which was prefaced by the remarks: 'To the magistrates and country gentlemen of England, Scotland and Ireland, these observations are respectfully addressed, by, their obedient humble servant, John Sidney'. According to his brother Samuel, John was a 'close observer, but no writer.'[54] As a result, they co-edited a number of articles and books together including *The Australian Handbook* (1848), followed by *Sidney's Emigrant's Journal* and *Three Colonies of Australia* (1852). He returned to Australia in 1848.

In 1850, John Sidney's 'Milking in Australia' was published in the first issue of *Household Words*. Nevertheless, John's contribution to *H.W.* continued indirectly, as his brother Samuel used information provided by

John as a source of the personal observations and experiences in the articles he wrote (see below).[55]
– 'Milking in Australia' (2).

Sidney, Samuel (1813–1883). The son of Abraham Solomon and like his brother John assumed the surname Sidney. Educated for the law, he worked as a solicitor for a time before turning to journalism and becoming a writer specialising on topics concerning emigration, railways and agriculture— chiefly, livestock. He co-authored a number of books and articles with his brother John (see, above), made speeches on emigration and wrote pamphlets on the subject. He also wrote for *Illustrated London News* as well as a number of journals relating to agriculture and stock. He was an assistant commissioner for the Great Exhibition. The Sidneys' *Australian Handbook* (1848) was extremely popular and sold thousands of copies; as did their *Sidney's Emigrant's Journal* (1848–50). In 1852, Samuel Sidney published *The Three Colonies of Australia*.

Samuel Sidney met Dickens as a result of the prominence he and his brother achieved through their books, pamphlets and speeches. They were regarded as authorities on migration to Australia which Dickens wanted to foster and encourage.

As an illustration of Dickens' desire to acquire accurate information about Australia, even before the discovery of gold, in a letter to Miss Burdette-Coutts, Dickens referred to 'the writers of those pamphlets', and stated that 'he had some time before directed a gentleman' to 'confer with them on the practicality of our doing something useful on the subject of emigration.' Dickens said the books they sent 'gave him knowledge of the state of society in New South Wales of which one could have no previous understanding, and which would seem to be quite misunderstood, or very little known, even in the cities of New South Wales itself.'[56]

Despite having never personally visited Australia, of the sixty articles Samuel Sidney wrote for *H.W.*, seventeen were about Australia. These had been augmented by the substantial correspondence received by Dickens and other members of staff from immigrants to Australia, and especially through personal information supplied by his brother John and others, such as Caroline Chisholm.

– 'Milking in Australia', John Sidney & Samuel Sidney (2); 'An Australian Ploughman's Story' (3); 'Two-Handed Dick the Stockman' (3); 'An Exploring Adventure' (3); 'Chip: Family Colonisation Loan Society' (2); 'Father Gabriel; or, The Fortunes of a Farmer' (3); 'Father Gabriel's Story' (3); 'Two Adventures at Sea' (5); 'Chip: Letter of Introduction to Sydney' (2); 'Christmas Day in the Bush' (3); 'Two Scenes in the Life of John Bodger' (2); 'Three Colonial Epochs' (2); 'Better Ties Than Red Tape' (2); 'Going to the Dogs' (3); 'Chip: What to Take to Australia' (2); 'Chip: Climate of Australia' (2); 'Lost and Found in the Gold Fields' (4); 'Treasures of the Deep' (5); 'Land ho!—Port Jackson' (2).

Thomas, William Moy (1828–1910) journalist, drama critic, novelist and scholar who studied law but soon turned to writing. Thomas contributed articles to numerous periodicals. He was the London correspondent for the *New York Round Table* and was on the staff of *Daily News*, and drama critic for the *Graphic* and *Academy* and other publications.

Lohrli wrote that Dickens was introduced to Thomas in 1850 and soon came to 'think highly of Thomas' ability and judgement.' Furthermore, in discussing Thomas' contribution to *H.W.* she said, 'The social purposes of Dickens' literary works was well understood by Thomas; nine years after Dickens' death he acclaimed and acknowledged Dickens in an article published in *Social Notes*, October 25, 1879.'[57]

Thomas was to write thirty-six articles over the next six years for *H.W.* The one article he wrote relating to Australia was 'Transported for Life'. It is an account of the transportation to Norfolk Island (then to Van Diemen's Land), of William Henry Barber (not named in the article). Barber, a solicitor, had been convicted of complicity in a case of fraud and forgery and had been transported in 1844; he had received a final unconditional pardon in 1848. Lohrli records that the basis of this article was 'probably based on the book *The Case of Mr. W.H. Barber'* and that Dickens had a copy in his library.

Thomas' article in *H.W.*, told in first person, is stated to have 'been taken down from the lips of the narrator, whose sufferings are described; with the object of shewing [sic] what Transportation, at the present time, really is.' Also that W.L. Clay, in (*The Prison Chaplain* p. 215n) referred to the article as 'a painfully interesting narrative' giving 'a good account of Norfolk Island' under the administration of Major Joseph Childs. Certain regulations as recorded in the article were no longer in force at the time it appeared in *Household Words*.[58]

– 'Transported For Life, Parts 1 and 2' (1).

Ullathorne, Rev. William B. The article 'The New Colonists of Norfolk Island', quotes Ullathorne's description of Norfolk Island from his *Catholic Mission in Australia*, first published in 1836. The occasion for reprinting the description was the government's removal, in 1856, of the inhabitants of Pitcairn Island to Norfolk Island. There is no record of who prepared this item for publication in *Household Words*.[59]

– 'The New Colonists of Norfolk Island' (1).

Vincent, Frank (Francis), exact details not recorded however the articles suggest he was born and educated in England, (date unknown). According to his *H.W.* article, Vincent migrated to the Port Phillip district of Australia, 'many years ago when Australia was a vast sheep-walk' and was 'unwilling to settle prematurely' but nevertheless, armed with letters of introduction to several squatters, 'took a tour from one station to another in what later became Victoria.' Eventually, Vincent settled at Gundagai, on the Murrumbidgee River, New South Wales, and brought his 'wife up from Sydney.'[60]

During one of his years of residence (date not firmly established) at Gundagai—'in the late evening of the last day of March,' a flood occurred that inundated the entire Gundagai valley that resulted in the 'loss of several lives.' Lohrli's noted 'there is a record, from 1844 to 1852 of several floods in the area, after which the settlement was moved to a higher site. The flood that is recorded in 'The Waters Are Out' is not the huge flood of June 1852 "the great flood" that resulted in the loss of more than a hundred lives.' The latest date in which the writer mentions in connection with his residence in Australia is 1853, when he visited the goldfields of Victoria.

The *H.W.* office book records payment was made to a Bristol address, in February 1858. So he must have left Australia no later than the latter months of 1857, although he may well have returned to Australia. As Lohrli notes, the *Sands' Country Directory and Gazette of NSW* for 1881–82, (in the Mitchell Library) 'lists a Frank Vincent, newspaper proprietor of Uralla, in the Gundagai district.' She suggests this may have been the *H.W.* contributor.[61]
– 'Coo-ee!' (3); 'John Chinaman in Australia', F. Vincent & Morley (2); 'Australian Jim Walker' (3); 'The Waters Are Out' (3).

Weir, William (1802–1858), lawyer, journalist; educated at Ayr Academy, Scotland and at University of Göttingen. Weir was called to the Scottish bar in 1827 and later became the first editor of the Glasgow *Argus* before moving to London. He contributed to the *Spectator* and was engaged on the staff of the *Daily News* by Dickens where he served as the paper's 'chief authority on railways and commercial affairs'.[62]

Weir contributed four articles to *H.W.* on commerce and transport, literature and law. Whilst not primarily focused on Australia, the two articles included in this collection (written at the advent of steam ships), relate to the pressing needs to develop faster international shipping routes. They highlight the necessity for the Panama and Suez Canals to be built, to thus transform global transport, including shipping to Australia.
– 'Short Cuts Across the Globe: The Panama Canal' (5); 'Short Cuts Across the Globe: The Isthmus of Suez', Weir & W. H. Wills (5).

Whitty, Edward Michael (1827–1860). Whitty was the son of a newspaper editor and was educated at Liverpool Institute, and in Hanover. In 1846 he was a writer in the provincial press. In 1848–49 he wrote the parliamentary summaries for *The Times* and some of his summaries were published in *History of the Sessions 1852–3: A Parliamentary Retrospect*, and in *Governing Classes of Great Britain: Political Portraits*, both published 1854. He was editor of *Northern Whig* in 1857–58.

Whitty died in 1860, having migrated to Melbourne (date uncertain) to work on the Melbourne *Argus*.

'Post To Australia' (April, 1856) is a criticism of the lack of interest the British government had in commerce and trade, and the government's failure to re-establish steamship services (to Australia) that had been discontinued during the Crimean War.[63] Whitty wrote, 'for mercy's sake lets get circumnavigation discussions out of the Circumlocution Office as fast as possible.'

The theme of circumlocution was to be used by Dickens in *H.W.* in an article entitled, 'Nobody, Somebody and Everybody', (30 August 1856) which was directed at the maladministration of the country, and in particular of the Crimean War. The 'Circumlocution Office' emerged again as a major focus of his novel *Little Dorritt*, (which was originally to be called Nobody's Fault). In reference to Dickens' writing, author Peter Ackroyd noted that the notion of circumlocution was to become: 'the whole vast babble of the world, the world of travellers, the world of hypocrisy, [and] the world of imprisonment.'[64] – 'Post to Australia' (5).

Wills, William Henry (1810–1880), journalist, sub-editor of *H.W.* and later (when it continued under the re-named banner), *All The Year Round*. William Wills was the son of a wealthy shipowner who died when William was quite young. As a result Wills' education was limited, as he was required to financially support his family. He turned to journalism and contributed to several periodicals including, *Penny Magazine*, *Saturday Magazine*, *McCulloch's Geographical Dictionary* and *Bentley's Miscellany*. Wills was one of the original literary staff members of *Punch* and contributed to its first issue in 1841. In 1841 he became assistant editor of *Chambers' Journal*, a post he held until 1845.

He married Janet Chambers, and in that same year became Dickens' personal secretary, with the responsibility of helping Dickens to found and edit *Daily News*. He continued to do so until 1849 (even though Dickens had quit *Daily News*). Dickens asked him to be the assistant editor of *Household Words*. Dickens, Forster, Bradbury, Evans and Wills became joint proprietors of *H.W.* (with Wills holding only a small share) on an annual income of £420 per annum, compared to Dickens' £500 pa.

William Wills contributed to 129 issues of *H.W.*, and wrote twenty-eight full-length articles in the first volume alone, but increasingly over the years left more of the writing to other contributors. Nevertheless he wrote or co-wrote a further 178 articles, as well as contributing to many more, in his editing capacity. In the course of his writings, Stone wrote, 'he collaborated with Dickens' more than any other writer.'[65]

Wills was equally responsible with Dickens for the editorial policy and, although *Household Words* bore Dickens' name, in the public's eye Wills' name was nevertheless closely associated. Wills had the responsibility of careful handling of the business transactions of *H.W.*, something to which Dickens was largely indifferent. Wills 'was also responsible for the day-to-day management of the editorial office, carrying on correspondence, conferring with the printers and with contributors and delegating some of the assignments. He referred to Dickens those articles that required Dickens' final decision, and kept the Office Book—a record of items published in *H.W.*, with the amount paid for contributed items.'[66]

Items with an Australian connection that Wills was involved in writing are listed below.

– 'Short Cuts Across the Globe: The Panama Canal', William Weir & Wills (5); 'Short Cuts Across the Globe: The Isthmus of Suez', William Weir & Wills (5); 'Two Letters from Australia', Francis Gwynne & Wills (3); 'Chip: Easy Spelling and Hard Reading', Miss Cox & Wills (2); 'Chip: Safety for Female Immigrants' (2); 'Chip: The Bush Fire Extinguisher', Correspondent & Wills (3); 'Chip: A Golden Newspaper', William Thomas Keene & Wills (4); 'Chip: Official Emigration' (2); 'Chip: Transported for Life' (1); 'First Stage to Australia', Wills & John Capper (2).

Notes

[1] Lohrli, p. 476.

[2] *Australian Dictionary of Biography*, Vol. 4, 1851–90, pp. 221–23.

[3] Lohrli, p. 227.

[4] Lohrli, pp. 226–28.

[5] *Australian Dictionary of Biography*, Vol. 1, p. 222.

[6] Ackroyd, p. 622.

[7] Forster, p. 703.

[8] Murray, p. 68.

[9] Letters of the Dickens Family 1870–1913, National Library of Australia, Manuscripts MS2563.

[10] Lohrli, pp. 269–70.

[11] Lohrli, pp. 290–91.

[12] Lohrli, pp. 303–04.

[13] Lohrli, p. 309.

[14] Lohrli, p. 309.

[15] *Australian Dictionary of Biography*, Vol. 4, 1851–90, p. 424.

[16] Finnane, p. 26.

[17] Keesing, p. 3.

[18] Keesing, p. 56.

[19] Keesing, p. 401.

[20] *Australian Dictionary of Biography*, Vol. 4, 1851–90, pp. 435–36.

[21] Keesing, pp. 401–02.

[22] Lohrli, p. 315.

[23] Lohrli, p. 322.

[24] Gordon, Harry, *An Eyewitness History of Australia*, pp. 55–61.

[25] Lohrli, p. 330.

[26] *Australian Dictionary of Biography*, Vol. 5, 1851–90, pp. 239–40.

[27] *Australian Dictionary of Biography*, Vol. 5, 1851–90, pp. 239–40.

[28] Lohrli, p. 337.

[29] Lohrli, p. 352.

[30] *Australian Dictionary of Biography*, Vol. 5, 1851–90, pp. 239–40.

[31] Lohrli, p. 366.

[32] Significant Tasmanian Women Project, Dept of Premier and Cabinet, Tasmania, www.dpac.tas.gov.au/divisions/cdd/women/leadership/significant_tasmanian_women.

[33] Barber, W.H. *The case of Mr W.H. Barber... : Convicted in 1844 of a Supposed Guilty Knowledge of Certain Will Forgeries, Consisting of His Memorial to Sir James Graham and Other Documents Establishing ... His Perfect Innocence ... with Editorial Remarks* / by Archibald Michie [Sydney?: s.n.], 1847 (Sydney: Kemp and Fairfax).

[34] Lohrli, p. 445.

[35] *Australian Dictionary of Biography*, Vol. 5, 1851–90, pp. 246–48.

[36] Mary Lazarus, *A Tale of Two Brothers: Charles Dickens's Sons in Australia*, p. 19.

[37] Lohrli, p. 367.

[38] *Australian Dictionary of Biography*, Vol.5, 1851–90, pp. 246–48.

[39] Lohrli, p. 367.

[40] Lohrli, p. 370.

[41] Lohrli, p. 370.

[42] Lohrli, p. 380.

[43] Lohrli, p. 380.

[44] Pers. Comm.., Assoc. Prof. E.B. Joyce—School of Earth Sciences, Melbourne University.

[45] Lohrli, pp. 389–90.

[46] Lohrli, p. 390.

[47] Lohrli, p. 390.

[48] Lohrli, p. 399.

[49] Flannery, p. 230.

[50] Lohrli, p. 411.

[51] Stone, p. 659.

[52] Forster, p. 558.

[53] Flannery, p. 326.

[54] Lohrli, p. 429.

[55] Lohrli, p. 429.

[56] Lohrli, p. 430.

[57] Lohrli, pp. 445–46.

[58] Lohrli, p. 446.

[59] Lohrli, p. 479.

[60] Lohrli, p. 452.

[61] Lohrli, p. 452.

[62] Lohrli, p. 455.
[63] Lohrli, p. 460.
[64] Ackroyd, p. 786.
[65] Stone, p. 660.
[66] Lohrli, pp. 460–65.

Bibliography

Australian Dictionary of Biography 1851–1890, Vols. 4 & 5, various eds. Melbourne: Melbourne University Press, 1969–1976.

Ackroyd, Peter, *Dickens*, London: Minerva Paperback, 1991.

Bate, Weston, *Victorian Gold Rushes*, Ringwood, Vic.: Mcphee Gribble /Penguin Books, 1988.

Blainey, Geoffrey, *The Rush that Never Ended: a History of Australian Mining*, Melbourne: Melbourne University Press, 1981.

Brown, Ivor, In E.W.F. Tomlin (Ed.), *Charles Dickens 1812–1870: A Century Volume*, London: Weidenfeld and Nicolson Ltd., 1969.

Chesterton, G.K., *Charles Dickens*, London: Methuen & Co. 1906.

Cannon, Michael, *Who's Master? Who's Man? Australia in the Victorian Age*, Melbourne: Currey O'Neil, 1982.

_____, *Life in the Country: Australia in the Victorian Age 2*, Melbourne: Currey O'Neil Ross, 1983.

Fido, Martin, *Charles Dickens: An Authentic Account of His Life and Times*, Sydney: The Hamlyn Publishing Group Ltd. n.d.

Finnane, Mark, (Ed.), *The Difficulties of My Position: The Diaries of Prison Governor John Buckley Castieau, 1855–1884*, Canberra: The National Library of Australia, 2004.

Flannery, Tim, (Ed.), *The Birth of Melbourne*, Melbourne: Text Publishing, 2004.

Hancock, Marguerite, (Ed.), *Glimpses of Life in Victoria by 'A Resident'*, Melbourne: The Miegunyah Press, 1996.

Hobsbawm, Eric, *The Age of Capital: 1848–1875*, London: Abacus, 2003.

Hobsbaum, Philip, *A Reader's Guide to Charles Dickens*, London: Thames and Hudson, 1977.

Household Words, 1850–1859, Volumes 1–19, London: Bradbury and Evans, (Vols. 1–3, 5, 7, 11, 17–18), 1850–1858; New York: McElrath & Barker, (Vols. 7–16), 1853–1858; New York: Fredric Brady, (Vol. 19), 1859.

Hughes, Robert, *The Fatal Shore: a History of the Transportation of Convicts to Australia 1787–1868*, London: The Harvill Press, 1986.

Forster, John, *The Life of Charles Dickens, Fireside Edition*, New York: Oxford University Press, n. d.

Johnston, Judith & Anderson, Monica, *Australia Imagined: Views from the British Periodical Press, 1800–1900*, Crawley: University of Western Australia Press, 2005.

Keesing, Nancy (Ed.), *History of the Australian Gold Rushes: By Those Who Were There*, North Ryde, NSW: Angus and Robertson, 1987.

Lohrli, Anne, *Household Words: Table of Contents, List of Contributors and Their Contributions*, Toronto: University of Toronto Press, 1973.

Murray, Brian, *Charles Dickens*, New York: Continuum, 1994.

Pope-Hennessy, Una, *Charles Dickens 1812–1870*, London: Reprint Society, 1947.

Ryan, J.S. & Reed, A.H., *Charles Dickens and New Zealand*, Wellington: A.H. & A.W. Reed, 1965.

Sanderson, Edgar, *The British Empire in the Nineteenth Century,* Vol. VI, London: Blackie & Son, 1898.

Smiley, Jane, *Charles Dickens*, London, Phoenix Paperback, 2003.

Stone, Harry, *Charles Dickens' Uncollected Writings from Household Words, 1850–1859,*Volumes 1 & 2, Bloomington, Indiana: University of Indiana Press, 1968.

Ward, Russel, *Australia Since the Coming of Man*, Sydney: Lansdowne Press, 1982.

Webster's New Twentieth Century Dictionary of the English Language, Unabridged, New York: The World Publishing Company, 1971.

Webster's Third New International Dictionary, Unabridged, Springfield, Mass: Merriam Webster Inc. 1993.

Welles Henderson, J., *Jack Tar: A Sailor's Life 1750–1910*, Woodbridge: Antique Collectors' Club, 1999.

Wilson, Angus, *The Words of Charles Dickens*, London: Martin Secker & Warburg, 1970.

Charles Dickens' Australia
Selected essays from *Household Words*
1850–1859

Researched and presented by Margaret Mendelawitz

Book One: *Convict Stories*, ISBN 9781920898670
Book Two: *Immigration*, ISBN 9781920898687
Book Three: *Frontier Stories*, ISBN 9781920898694
Book Four: *Mining and Gold*, ISBN 9781920899257
Book Five: *Maritime Conditions*, ISBN 9781920899264
Five-Volume Set: ISBN 9781920899271